A Field Guide to the Wild Orchids of Thailand

Third and Expanded Edition

by

Nantiya Vaddhanaphuti

SILKWORM BOOKS

Third and Expanded Edition in 2001
by
Silkworm Books
104/5 Chiang Mai-Hot Road, T. Suthep A. Muang Chiang Mai 50100, Thailand
E-mail: silkworm@pobox.com

Silkworm Books is a registered trademark of
Trasvin Publications Limited Partnership

Set in Garamond 10 pt. and 55 Helvetica Roman 8 pt.
Printed in Thailand by O.S. Printing House, Bangkok

To

Dr. Gunnar Seidenfaden

Acknowledgments

This book has been completed through the collaboration of several friends who have been collecting both common and rare species of our native orchids. I am grateful for their generosity in sharing some of these specimens with me. Without them, my work would have been incomplete.

I propose that this book be a modest supplement to Dr. Gunnar Seidenfaden's fourteen-volume work, *Orchid Genera in Thailand,* which I have relied on as my main reference. I am very grateful to Dr. Seidenfaden for his support for my work.

To him, I dedicate this book.

Nantiya Vaddhanaphuti
Chiang Mai
May 2000

Contents

Introduction

Orchids have their own unique characteristics and charms. The mere fact that their roots live on air is enough to make us wonder how they can sustain themselves. The roots of the orchid are different from those of other plants, consisting of a special sponge-like layer of tissues called velamen that covers up the true roots inside. This special sheathing acts as a moisture-collecting device while protecting the roots underneath from direct sunlight. The orchid's green leaves play the actual role of food manufacturing. Orchids are epiphytes, that is, the roots' main duty is to grasp and cling to other larger structures such as trees, without in any way harming or taking away food from the host, unlike a parasitic plant. Some orchids have roots that go into the ground like most other plants, while others find more unusual places to grow such as in the crevices of rocks on the side of a cliff.

Orchids are monocotyledonous plants and have two different types of growth structures. One is to grow from the vegetative apex (monopodial), an example being the *Vanda coerulea*. The other is to grow out horizontally (sympodial), sending pseudobulbs up from the rhizome. The new shoots will collect and replenish the old ones with food. Orchids that grow in this fashion are, for instance, *Dendrobium chrysotoxum*.

The flowers are what clearly distinguishes one orchid from another. Some orchids bear large flowers of bright hues, and some have smaller or even tiny flowers of softer tones. They may flower singly or in small groups of two or three per stem. Others will bloom in a big cluster or a bunch, with some standing up on an erect stem and others bending down in a flowing cluster. Some have flowers that bloom in alternating sequences and take quite a few days to wither, while some bloom and wither at the same time and do not last as long. The scent of orchids also differs, ranging from no smell, to a soft and subtle scent, to a full-bodied and pungent fragrance.

Each orchid flower has two sets of petals consisting of three outer and three inner petals. The three inner petals will usually consist of an identical pair and a singular one with distinctive features both in shape and color. This single petal, which most often will be brighter in color, is called the "lip" or "labellum". The pouch-shaped lip of the Lady Slipper orchid usually looks like the toe of a shoe. The three outer petals are generally smaller and do not have as vivid a color as the inner petals. They may also have a pair with an identical look and a singular one like the inner petals, or all three of them may look the same.

Inside the blooms are the stylis with the stigma, fused with the filament and anther. The pollinia—the mass of pollen—has the appearance of a tightly squeezed clump of wax. When the pollen comes in contact with the stigma, the bloom will rapidly wither and the ovary located at the base will expand into a pod, which will take from six months to one year to ripen. As maturity peaks, the full-grown pod will burst open longitudinally and the mass of minuscule seeds inside will be distributed into the air. Some of these pods can contain millions of seeds. The seeds will be airborne until, with great luck, some land on a spot of a host tree which happens to be covered with a kind of fungi called mycorrhiza which is essential in supplying food during the first part of the seedling's growth until it can mature into another orchid plant.

Most wild orchids bloom only once a year. Those that do so more than once are rare. The times of year that certain orchids bloom vary. *Rhyncstylis gigantea* begins flowering in December and January, while the clustered orchids of *Dendrobium aggregatum*, *Dendrobium chrysotoxum* and *Dendrobium thyrsiflorum* usually bloom in February and March. The *Rhyncostylis retusa* follows in April and May right along with *Aerides odorata*, *Aerides falcata* and *Aerides multiflora*. July and August is the time for *Vanda coerulea*. These are only some of the more prominent and better-known ones. There are quite a lot more orchids that bloom at different periods throughout the year.

Wild orchids differ distinctly from cultivated orchids nowadays, particularly in size, shape and color. For example, the wild *Vanda coerulea* has a paler shade, the tesselation is not as clear and as vivid, and the petals are significantly more twisted (although at the same time retaining their natural beauty) than the *Vanda coerulea* sold in the market. Breeders have improved and altered those features by bringing in some specimens from the wild to cultivate, then using the process of either self-pollination or cross-pollination to develop hybrids. The seeds from the pods of these new "breeds" are then brought to the laboratory for further embryo culture, cultivation and selection to obtain the features desired. Generally the features sought by these processes are brighter colors, more obvious tesselation, and less twisted petals so that a circular form is achieved. Besides self-pollination and cross-pollination, the orchids are sometimes pollinated from orchids of different species and families in order to obtain other special features such as, in the case of *Vanda* sp. for example, producing flowers more than once a year.

Another distinct quality of the wild orchid is its vigor and resistance to disease and insects, plus its ability to withstand adverse environmental factors, and the fact that it can produce a great quantity of seeds at one time. In some cases, there is still a need to repollinate the already cultivated and hybridized orchids from wild orchids once more in order to regain some of the missing features in response to the market trends of the moment. So, it can be clearly seen that wild orchids are the source of essential features and play an important role in the continuing development and maintenance of healthy hybrids. Thus they should always be highly regarded and preserved with utmost care.

As mentioned earlier, most wild orchids flower only once a year and the form of their blooms are not those most popular on the market, so not many people raise them, except for enthusiasts of wild orchids who truly love their natural look, who may also raise them for experimental and hybridization purposes. We don't know how many of our Thai orchids have already become extinct, both from natural causes such as fungal diseases, insects or forest fires, and from human negligence. Not realizing the dangers of extinction, villagers and dealers are cooperating in collecting wild orchids from the forests in increasing number in order to supply the annually rising international demand for Thai wild orchids. It is to be hoped that the problem of wild orchid conservation, along with the conditions and problems faced by the existing forests, will stimulate interest and workable solutions, before it is too late. Although leaving the orchids in their own natural environment could be the best way to preserve them, a small number of orchids should perhaps be brought out from the forest for research or conservation purposes.

Our hope is that some of these Thai wild orchids may have already touched your heart and fascinated you with their forms and colors. Nature has given us these splendid plants. May the beauty of the wild orchid create in all of us a love for nature and for the Thai forests where they grow.

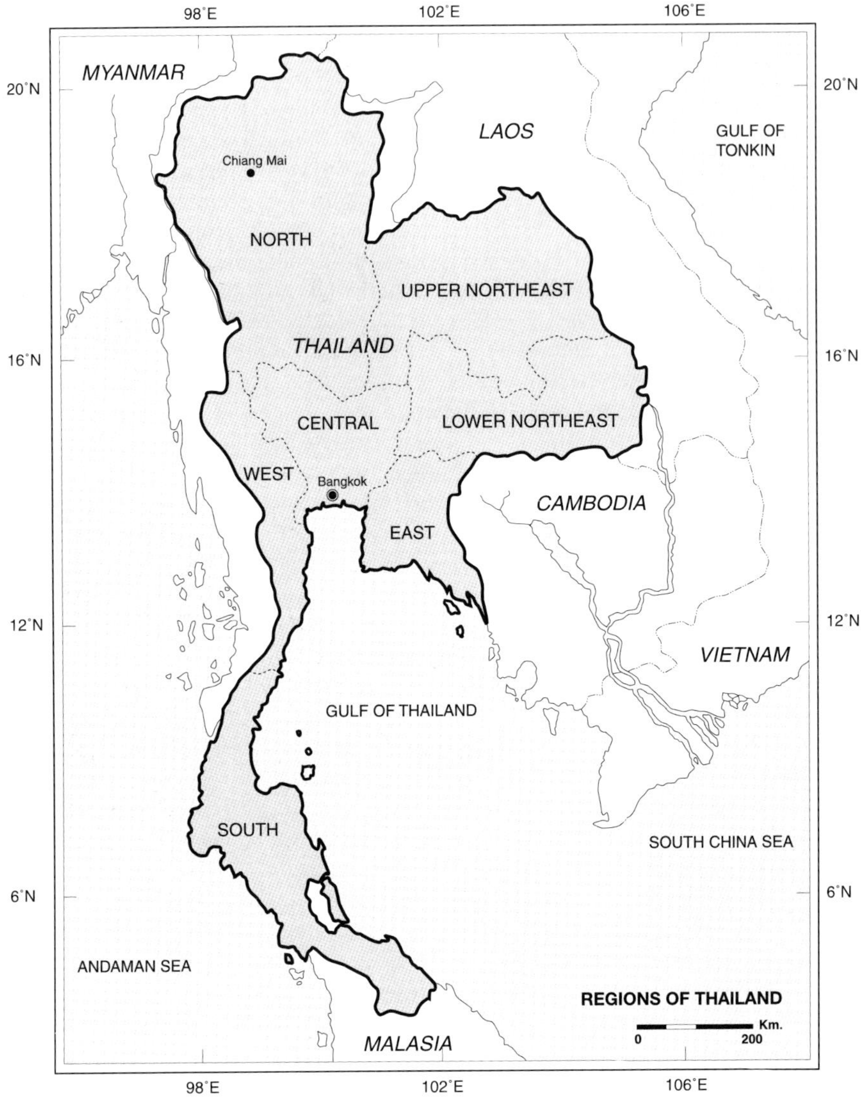
98°E
102°E
106°E
20°N
16°N
12°N
6°N
MYANMAR
LAOS
GULF OF
TONKIN
Chiang Mai
NORTH
UPPER NORTHEAST
THAILAND
CENTRAL
LOWER NORTHEAST
WEST
Bangkok
CAMBODIA
EAST
VIETNAM
GULF OF THAILAND
SOUTH
SOUTH CHINA SEA
ANDAMAN SEA
REGIONS OF THAILAND
Km.
0
200
MALASIA

1. *Acampe ochracea* (Lindl.) Hochr.

Thai name:–
Distribution: North, Upper Northeast, Central, East, South
Flowering period: November–December
Characteristics: Yellow sepals and petals with transverse brown bars, lip white with small purple dots. Inflorescence branching.
Size: 0.6 cm. wide and 0.8 cm. long
Number of flowers: 5–12

2. *Acampe papillosa* (Lindl.) Lindl.

Thai name: Chang Saraphi Noi ช้างสารภีน้อย
Distribution: North, Lower Northeast, West
Flowering period: November–January
Characteristics: Yellow flowers with brown spots, lip pure white with purple spots at the base. Inflorescence sub-umbellate.
Size: 0.8 cm.
Number of flowers: 10–12 flowers in one head
Scent: Fragrant

3. *Acampe rigida* (Buch.-Ham. ex J. E. Sm.) Hunt.

Thai name: Chang Saraphi, Uang Chet Poi ช้างสารภี, เอื้องเจ็ดปอย
Distribution: North, Upper Northeast, West, South
Flowering period: October–January
Characteristics: Brownish yellow flower with reddish brown stripes, midlobe of lip white.
Size: 1.5 cm., flowers dense in 7.5-cm. head
Number of flowers: 5–7
Scent: Fragrant

4. *Acampe thailandica* Seidenf.

Thai name:–
Distribution: North
Flowering period: April
Characteristics: Sepals and petals white with pink blotches medially, epichile of lip violet, hypochile white.
Size: 0.7 cm.
Number of flowers: 7–8

5. *Acanthephippium sylhetense* Lindl.

Thai name:–
Distribution: North, Lower Northeast, East, South
Flowering period: October
Characteristics: Sepal outside white, inside yellowish with red dots distally, midlobe and keels strong yellow, lateral sepals creamish basally, glossy red with some yellow apically.
Size: 2 cm. wide and 3.5 cm. long
Number of flowers: 1–3

6. *Acriopsis indica* Wight

Thai name: Kesa Phra Chao, Chuk Phram เกศาพระเจ้า, จุกพราหมณ์
Distribution: North, Northeast, East, South
Flowering period: February
Characteristics: Sepals and petals greenish yellow with purple dots, lip white.
Size: 0.8 cm.
Number of flowers: 10–15 per branch

7. *Acriopsis javanica* Reinw.

Thai name:–
Distribution: North, West, South
Flowering period: May, January
Characteristics: Sepals and petals greenish yellow with purple tips, lip white with purple center and two purple keels.
Size: 1.1 cm.
Number of flowers: 20

8. *Adenoncos major* Ridl.

Thai name:–
Distribution: West, South
Flowering period: December
Characteristics: Greenish sepals and petals, lip brownish with concave surface.
Size: 0.8 cm.
Number of flowers: 1

9. *Adenoncos parviflora* Ridl.

Thai name:–
Distribution: West, South
Flowering period: December
Characteristics: Brownish yellow sepals and petals with darker lip; lip has distinct sidelobes and light yellow cone on the center.
Size: 0.7 cm.
Number of flowers: 1

10. *Adenoncos sumatrana* J. J. Sm.

Thai name:–
Distribution: South
Flowering period: December
Characteristics: Yellowish green sepals and petals with dark green lip, distal part of lip surface concave.
Size: 0.4 cm.
Number of flowers: 3–4

11. *Aerides crassifolia* Par. ex Burb.

Thai name: Uang Kulap Daeng
เอื้องกุหลาบแดง
Distribution: North, Northeast, Central, West
Flowering period: April–May
Characteristics: Mauve flowers, lip dark mauve.
Size: 3 cm.
Number of flowers: 15–20

12. *Aerides falcata* Lindl.

Thai name: Uang Kulap Krapao Poet
เอื้องกุหลาบกระเป๋าเปิด
Distribution: Widely distributed
Flowering period: April–May
Characteristics: White sepals and petals blotched with light lavender, distal half of midlobe purple.
Size: 2.5 cm.
Number of flowers: 30
Scent: Highly fragrant

13. *Aerides flabellata* Rolfe ex Downie

Thai name: Uang Inthachak,
Uang Nok Phirap
เอื้องอินทจักร, เอื้องนกพิราบ
Distribution: North, Upper Northeast
Flowering period: April–May
Characteristics: Sepals and petals chartreuse with brown blotches and spots, lip white with purple blotches, throat and column tip yellow.
Size: 2 cm.
Number of flowers: 10–15

14. *Aerides houlettiana* Rchb. f.

Thai name: Uang Kulap Luang Korat
เอื้องกุหลาบเหลืองโคราช
Distribution: Northeast
Flowering period: April–May
Characteristics: Sepals and petals light yellow to yellow with a touch of lavender toward the tip, lip creamy white with a lavender blotch.
Size: 2.5 cm.
Number of flowers: 12–20
Scent: Fragrant

15. *Aerides krabiense* Seidenf.

Thai name: Uang Kulap Phuang Chomphu, Uang Kulap Krabi
เอื้องกุหลาบพวงชมพู, เอื้องกุหลาบกระบี่

Distribution: South

Flowering period: May

Characteristics: Purplish pink sepals and petals with darker colour at tip, midlobe of lip broad, rounded, obtuse.

Size: 2 cm.

Number of flowers: 20

16. *Aerides multiflora* Roxb.

Thai name: Uang Kulap Malai Daeng
เอื้องกุหลาบมาลัยแดง

Distribution: Widely distributed

Flowering period: April–May

Characteristics: Sepals and petals white, flushed with purple toward tip, purple-spotted toward base, lip purple.

Size: 2.5 cm.

Number of flowers: Up to 50

17. *Aerides odorata* Laur.

Thai name: Uang Kulap Krapao Pit
เอื้องกุหลาบกระเป๋าปิด
Distribution: North, Northeast, West, South
Flowering period: May
Characteristics: Sepals and petals white or very pale pink, blotched with light lavender at tips.
Size: 2.5 cm.
Number of flowers: Up to 30
Scent: Highly fragrant

18. *Aerides rosea* Lodd. ex Lindl. & Paxt.

Thai name: Uang Kulap Airawan, Uang Kulap Nan
เอื้องกุหลาบไอราวัณ, เอื้องกุหลาบน่าน
Distribution: North
Flowering period: May–June
Characteristics: Sepals and petals rose-purple with dark blotches and spots, middle of lip triangular acute.
Size: 1.5 cm.
Number of flowers: 20–25

19. *Agrostophyllum brevipes* King & Plantling

Thai name:–

Distribution: North, Northeast, West

Flowering period: May

Characteristics: Pink sepals and light yellow petals, operculum red.

Size: 0.5 cm.

Number of flowers: 6–7

20. *Agrostophyllum planicaule* (Wall. ex Lindl.) Rchb. f.

Thai name: Uang Pik Kai
เอื้องปีกไก่

Distribution: North, Central, East, South

Flowering period: June

Characteristics: Sepals and petals creamy white, lip white.

Size: 0.5 cm.

Number of flowers: 20 per head, bloom 1–2 at a time

21. *Anoechtochilus lanceolatus* Lindl.

Thai name: Nok Khum Fai
นกคุ้มไฟ

Distribution: North, Northeast

Flowering period: October–November

Characteristics: Bright yellow flower, epichile of lip with a V-shaped sinus between lobules.

Size: 0.5 cm. wide and 2.5 cm. long

Number of flowers: 7–10

22. *Anthogonium gracile* Wall. ex Lindl.

Thai name: Wan Phrao
ว่านพร้าว
Distribution: North, Northeast
Flowering period: October
Characteristics: White sepals and petals with purple lip.
Size: 1 cm.
Number of flowers: 10–12

23. *Aphyllorchis caudata* Rolfe

Thai name:–
Distribution: North
Flowering period: October
Characteristics: Creamy white sepals and petals with longitudinal brownish purple lines, lip dark brown.
Size: 2 cm. wide and 5 cm. long
Number of flowers: 25

24. *Appendicula anceps* Bl.

Thai name:–
Distribution: South
Flowering period: May–August
Characteristics: Sepals and petals greenish white, lip with two purple spots.
Size: 0.2 cm. wide and 0.3 cm. long
Number of flowers: 3–5

25. *Appendicula hexandra* (Koen) J. J. Sm.

Thai name:–
Distribution: East, South
Flowering period: May–August
Characteristics: Greenish white flower.
Size: 0.2 cm. wide and 0.3 cm long
Number of flowers: 2–3

26. *Appendicula pendula* Bl.

Thai name:–
Distribution: South
Flowering period: June
Characteristics: Greenish white flower, lip with reddish markings.
Size: 0.2 cm.
Number of flowers: 2–4

27. *Arachnis labrosa* (Lindl. & Paxt.) Rchb. f.

Thai name:–
Distribution: North, Upper Northeast, East
Flowering period: July
Characteristics: Sepals and petals greenish yellow with purplish brown markings, lip cream with red lines at base.
Size: 4–4.5 cm.
Number of flowers: Up to 10

28. *Arachnis limax* Seidenf.

Thai name:–
Distribution: North
Flowering period: August
Characteristics: Sepals and petals yellowish green with dark brown bars, lip reddish brown with purple tip, operculum yellow with purple flush.
Size: 4–4.5 cm.
Number of flowers: 1–3

29. *Arundina graminifolia* (D. Don) Hochr.

Thai name: Uang Phai
เอื้องไผ่
Distribution: Widely distributed, except Central Thailand
Flowering period: August–March
Characteristics: White to light lavender sepals and petals, lip has yellow center and dark purple apex with light purple stripes.
Size: 6–7 cm.
Number of flowers: 1–2

30. *Ascocentrum ampullaceum* (Roxb.) Schltr.

Thai name: Khem Muang
เข็มม่วง
Distribution: North, West
Flowering period: April
Characteristics: Mauve flowers, midlobe of lip linear-lanceolate.
Size: 1.2–1.5 cm.
Number of flowers: 20 or more

31. *Ascocentrum curvifolium* (Lindl.) Schltr.

Thai name: Khem Daeng
เข็มแดง
Distribution: North, East, West
Flowering period: March–April
Characteristics: Orange-red to red flowers, pure yellow is rare, apex of midlobe truncate-retuse.
Size: 1.5 cm.
Number of flowers: 20–25

32. *Ascocentrum miniatum* (Lindl.) Schltr.

Thai name: Khem Saet
เข็มแสด
Distribution: North, Northeast, East, South
Flowering period: February–April
Characteristics: Golden yellow to bright orange flower, midlobe elliptic.
Size: 1.5 cm.
Number of flowers: Up to 50

33. *Ascocentrum pusillum* Averyanov

Thai name:–
Distribution: Northeast
Flowering period: January
Characteristics: Reddish purple flower, lip dark purple, operculum white.
Size: 1.2 cm.
Number of flowers: 10

34. *Ascocentrum semiteretifolium* Seidenf.

Thai name: Khem Chomphu
เข็มชมพู
Distribution: North
Flowering period: February
Characteristics: Violet flowers with yellow sidelobes.
Size: 1 cm.
Number of flowers: Up to 10

35. *Bletilla sinensis* (Rolfe) Schltr.

Thai name:–
Distribution: North
Flowering period: January–February
Characteristics: Sepals and petals white with purple tip, lip white with purple spots and purple tip.
Size: 2.5–3 cm.
Number of flowers: 3

36. *Brachycorythis acuta* (Rchb. f.) Summerh.

Thai name:–
Distribution: North, Lower Northeast, Central, East, West
Flowering period: July
Characteristics: Sepals and petals green, lip light green with two brownish purple lines at base.
Size: 1 cm. wide and 2.5 cm. long
Number of flowers: 1

37. *Brachycorythis helferi* (Rchb. f.) Summerh.

Thai name: Thao Khulu, Mangkon Khap Kaeo
ท้าวคูลู, มังกรคาบแก้ว
Distribution: North, Central, East, South
Flowering period: July–September
Characteristics: White flower, large purple lip with white splash and yellow base.
Size: 3 cm.
Number of flowers: Up to 15

38. *Brachycorythis henryi* (Rchb. f.) Summerh.

Thai name: Wan Nang Bua Pong
ว่านนางบัวป้อง
Distribution: North
Flowering period: August
Characteristics: Purplish flower with big round, light purplish pink lip.
Size: 2.3 cm.
Number of flowers: 1

39. *Brachypeza laotica* (Seidenf.) Seidenf.

Thai name:–
Distribution: Central
Flowering period: December
Characteristics: Pinkish yellow sepals and petals, midlobe of lip with fine purple lines inside, lip creamy white.
Size: 2.5 cm.
Number of flowers: 3–4 blooms at a time

40. *Bromheadia aporoides* Rchb. f.

Thai name:–
Distribution: North, Upper Northeast, West
Flowering period: July
Characteristics: White flower, midlobe of lip white with yellow centre, sidelobes with purple stripes.
Size: 2 cm.
Number of flowers: 2–3

41. *Bulbophyllum affine* Lindl.

Thai name:–
Distribution: North, Upper Northeast
Flowering period: April–June
Characteristics: Sepals and petals yellow with reddish brown stripes, lip orange.
Size: 3 cm.
Number of flowers: 1

42. *Bulbophyllum alcicorne* Par. & Rchb. f.

Thai name:–
Distribution: North, West, South
Flowering period: June–August
Characteristics: Reddish brown sepals and petals, lip yellow.
Size: 0.4 cm.
Number of flowers: 10–12

43. *Bulbophyllum allenkerrii* Seidenf.

Thai name: Singto Hua Kalok
สิงโตหัวกะโหลก
Distribution: North
Flowering period: August–September
Characteristics: Sepals and petals yellow dotted purple, flower bract white striped with purple.
Size: 0.8 cm.
Number of flowers: 5-cm.-long inflorescence

44. *Bulbophyllum angusteelipticum* Seidenf.

Thai name:–
Distribution: North
Flowering period: June
Characteristics: Sepals brownish yellow, petals black purple with white ciliae, lip narrowly elliptic, purple black with very short hairs along edges and furrow.
Size: 1.5 cm.
Number of flowers: 10

45. *Bulbophyllum bisetum* Lindl.

Thai name:–
Distribution: North
Flowering period: August
Characteristics: Light green flowers with purple stripes, lip white hairy with purple central cavity.
Size: 0.6 cm.
Number of flowers: 3–7

46. *Bulbophyllum blepharistes* Rchb. f.

Thai name: Singto Samo Hin
สิงโตสมอหิน
Distribution: North, Northeast, Central, South
Flowering period: June–November
Characteristics: Greenish yellow sepals and petals, petals obtuse truncate with long ciliae.
Size: 1 cm. wide and 3 cm. long
Number of flowers: 5–10

47. *Bulbophyllum capillipes* Par. & Rchb. f.

Thai name:–
Distribution: North, Northeast
Flowering period: March
Characteristics: Sepals and petals yellowish green with brownish stripes, lip brown with red base.
Size: 1.3 cm.
Number of flowers: 1

48. *Bulbophyllum comosum* Collett & Hemsley

Thai name:–
Distribution: North
Flowering period: December–January
Characteristics: Creamy white bottle-brushed inflorescence.
Size: 0.3 cm. wide and 1.4 cm. long
Number of flowers: 5-cm.-long inflorescence
Scent: Coumarin-scented

49. *Bulbophyllum coniferum* Ridl.

Thai name:–
Distribution: North
Flowering period: July
Characteristics: Sepals and petals pale green with purple stripes, lip creamy white.
Size: 0.2 cm. wide and 0.4 cm. long
Number of flowers: 12–13-cm.-long inflorescence

50. *Bulbophyllum craibianum* Kerr.

Thai name:–
Distribution: North
Flowering period: September
Characteristics: Sepals and petals light yellow with orange yellow tip, apex of lip minutely retuse.
Size: 0.6 cm.
Number of flowers: 2–3

51. *Bulbophyllum dayanum* Rchb. f.

Thai name:–
Distribution: Upper Northeast, East, South
Flowering period: October
Characteristics: Brownish purple flowers, sepals and petals ciliated at edges.
Size: 2 cm.
Number of flowers: 2–5

52. *Bulbophyllum dissitiflorum* Seidenf.

Thai name:–
Distribution: Northeast
Flowering period: January
Characteristics: Brownish purple flowers with darker brown veins. Inflorescence long and drooping.
Size: 0.5 cm.
Number of flowers: 15–20

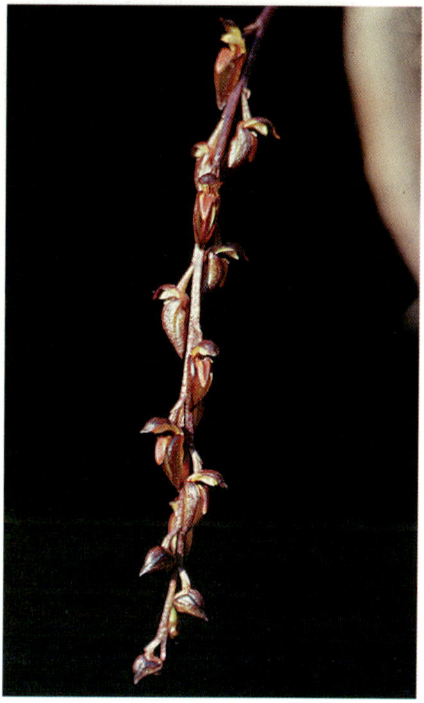

53. *Bulbophyllum gracillimum* (Rolfe) Rolfe

Thai name: Khon Ta Daeng
ขนตาแดง
Distribution: South
Flowering period: October–December
Characteristics: Purplish red flowers, apex of petals and dorsal sepal with long threads.
Size: 0.3 cm. wide and 2.5 cm. long
Number of flowers: 10–15

54. *Bulbophyllum gyrochilum* Seidenf.

Thai name:–

Distribution: North

Flowering period: March–June

Characteristics: Coral red flowers, lip strongly recurved with stiff hairs along edges.

Size: Dorsal sepals 4–4.5 mm., slightly shorter than or equal to lateral sepals.

Number of flowers: 8–10

55. *Bulbophyllum hirtum* (J. E. Sm.) Lindl.

Thai name: Uang Khon Ta Singto, Uang Kip Ma Khao
เอื้องขนตาสิงโต, เอื้องกีบม้าขาว

Distribution: North, Upper Northeast, West

Flowering period: December–April

Characteristics: Greenish white flowers, petals ovate, fimbriated at edges, lip greenish with yellowish brown tip.

Size: 0.8 cm.

Number of flowers: 12.5-cm.-long inflorescence

56. *Bulbophyllum kanburiense* Seidenf.

Thai name: Singto Muang Kan
สิงโตเมืองกาญจน์
Distribution: North, West
Flowering period: February
Characteristics: Pinkish white flowers with thin triangular floral bracts.
Size: 0.4 cm. wide and 2.2 cm. long
Number of flowers: 30

57. *Bulbophyllum khaoyaiense* Seidenf.

Thai name: Singto Khao Yai
สิงโตเขาใหญ่
Distribution: Lower Northeast
Flowering period: February
Characteristics: Brownish yellow lateral sepals, lip purple on upper side and white on lower side.
Size: 0.4 cm. wide and 2 cm. long
Number of flowers: 5–6

58. *Bulbophyllum khasyanum* Griff.

Thai name:–
Distribution: North, Upper Northeast
Flowering period: October
Characteristics: Blackish red oblong ovoid inflorescence.
Size: 0.3 cm.
Number of flowers: 2-cm.-long inflorescence

59. *Bulbophyllum lasiochilum* Par. & Rchb. f.

Thai name: Singto Nak Klam
สิงโตนักกล้าม
Distribution: North, Northeast, West, South
Flowering period: November–December
Characteristics: Lateral sepals pale yellow with dark red markings, petals with fine hairs at edges, lip greenish yellow with long ciliae at edges.
Size: 1.2 cm. wide and 3.2 cm. long
Number of flowers: 1

60. *Bulbophyllum laxiflorum* (Bl.) Lindl.

Thai name:–
Distribution: North, East, South
Flowering period: September
Characteristics: Light yellow sepals and petals, lip white.
Size: 0.5 cm. wide and 1.8 cm. long
Number of flowers: 14–15

61. *Bulbophyllum lindleyanum* Griff.

Thai name: Singto Lindley
สิงโตลินด์เลย์
Distribution: South
Flowering period: January
Characteristics: Flowers green with longitudinal dark brown stripes, sepals ciliated on surface, petals ciliated at edges.
Size: 0.4 cm.
Number of flowers: 15

62. *Bulbophyllum longipes* Rchb. f.

Thai name:–
Distribution: North
Flowering period: January
Characteristics: Light greenish yellow flowers with long pedicels, petals very small, lip strong yellow.
Size: 1.3 cm.
Number of flowers: 6–7

63. *Bulbophyllum longissimum* (Ridl.) Ridl.

Thai name:–
Distribution: South
Flowering period: January
Characteristics: Sepals and petals creamy white, lip yellow, dorsal sepal minutely ciliated at edges.
Size: 5 cm. long
Number of flowers: 3–4

64. *Bulbophyllum macranthum* Lindl.

Thai name: Singto Kam Pu Yai
สิงโตก้ามปูใหญ่
Distribution: Upper Northeast, Central, East, South
Flowering period: April
Characteristics: Sepals and petals creamy white with purple spots, lip yellowish white.
Size: 3.5 cm.
Number of flowers: 1

65. *Bulbophyllum macrocoleum* Seidenf.

Thai name:–
Distribution: North, Lower Northeast
Flowering period: November
Characteristics: Light straw yellow with a light brownish copper tint and with three purple brownish stripes on sepals, petals purple along edges, lip yellowish brown with yellow tip.
Size: 0.3 cm. wide and 0.8 cm. long
Number of flowers: 8-cm.-long inflorescence

66. *Bulbophyllum medusae* (Lindl.) Rchb. f.

Thai name: Singto Khao
สิงโตขาว
Distribution: South
Flowering period: October–November
Characteristics: White flower with orange yellow lip.
Size: 0.5 cm. wide and 6–7 cm. long, 5 cm. across inflorescence
Number of flowers: 10 or more

67. *Bulbophyllum moniliforme* Par. & Rchb. f.

Thai name: Singto Khai Pla
สิงโตไข่ปลา
Distribution: South
Flowering period: November
Characteristics: Orange sepals and petals with brownish orange longitudinal stripes, lip dark orange.
Size: 0.2 cm.
Number of flowers: 1

68. *Bulbophyllum morphologlorum* Krzl.

Thai name:–
Distribution: North, Upper Northeast
Flowering period: February
Characteristics: Greenish yellow flower with small purple dots, lip yellow with brownish edge along yellow median line.
Size: 0.2 cm.
Number of flowers: 0.5-wide and 1-cm.-long inflorescence

69. *Bulbophyllum muscarirubrum* Seidenf.

Thai name:–
Distribution: North, Upper Northeast, West
Flowering period: January–February
Characteristics: Sepals light reddish purple with darker dots, lip dark red.
Size: 0.3 cm. wide and 0.5 cm. long
Number of flowers: 10–15

70. *Bulbophyllum odoratissimum* (J. E. Sm.) Lindl.

Thai name: Singto Lot Fai
สิงโตหลอดไฟ
Distribution: North, Upper Northeast, East, West, South
Flowering period: May–June
Characteristics: Whitish yellow sepals, white petals and orange lip.
Size: 0.7 cm.
Number of flowers: 10–20

71. *Bulbophyllum orectopetalum* Garay et al.

Thai name:–
Distribution: Widely distributed
Flowering period: May–July
Characteristics: Yellow sepals and petals with red-brown veins and tesselated, lip with red-purple tint and dots. Dorsal sepal about 2 cm. long.
Size: 3.5–4 cm.
Number of flowers: 1

72. *Bulbophyllum patens* King ex Hk. f.

Thai name: Singto Kam Pu Daeng
สิงโตก้ามปูแดง
Distribution: South
Flowering period: November–December
Characteristics: Sepals and petals densely purple-spotted or completely purple, lip straight.
Size: 3.2 cm.
Number of flowers: 1

73. *Bulbophyllum pectinatum* Finet

Thai name:–
Distribution: North
Flowering period: July
Characteristics: Light yellow sepals and petals with purple stripes, lip light yellow with many small reddish dots.
Size: 3.5 cm.
Number of flowers: 1

74. *Bulbophyllum penicillium* Par. & Rchb. f.

Thai name: Singto Khrao Dam
สิงโตเคราดำ
Distribution: West
Flowering period: April
Characteristics: Light green sepals and petals with brownish purple lines, lip hairy, blackish purple.
Size: 1 cm.
Number of flowers: 15

75. *Bulbophyllum polyrhizum* Lindl.

Thai name:–
Distribution: North
Flowering period: February
Characteristics: Greenish yellow sepals and petals, lip strong yellow with brownish tint.
Size: 0.5 cm.
Number of flowers: 3–6

76. *Bulbophyllum propinquum* Krzl.

Thai name:–
Distribution: North, Lower Northeast
Flowering period: August–December
Characteristics: Purple flower with purple lip and a yellow median line.
Size: 0.4 cm. wide and 0.8 cm. long
Number of flowers: 3-cm.-long inflorescence

77. *Bulbophyllum purpurascens* Teijsm. & Binnend

Thai name:–
Distribution: South
Flowering period: March
Characteristics: Whitish yellow flowers, lip yellow.
Size: 0.4 cm. wide and 1.2 cm. long
Number of flowers: 6–8

78. *Bulbophyllum repens* Griff.

Thai name:–
Distribution: North
Flowering period: April
Characteristics: Greenish white sepals and petals with purple stripes, lip greenish yellow with purple median line.
Size: 0.2 cm. wide and 0.4 cm. long
Number of flowers: 1.5 cm. dense head

79. *Bulbophyllum rufilabrum* Par. ex Hooker f.

Thai name:–
Distribution: South
Flowering period: October
Characteristics: Greenish sepals and petals with dense blackish purple dots, lip reddish purple.
Size: 0.3 cm. wide and 0.6 cm. long
Number of flowers: 10–12

80. *Bulbophyllum rufinum* Rchb. f.

Thai name: Uang Kip Ma Yai
เอื้องกีบม้าใหญ่
Distribution: North, Northeast, East, South
Flowering period: October
Characteristics: Yellow flowers with purple stripes, lip dark yellow, rachis green, sometimes purple.
Size: 0.3 cm. wide and 0.8 cm. long
Number of flowers: 8-cm.-long inflorescence

81. *Bulbophyllum rugosisepalum* Seidenf.

Thai name:–
Distribution: Lower Northeast
Flowering period: January
Characteristics: Light greenish yellow sepals and petals with reddish purple glossy lip.
Size: 0.6 cm. wide and 3.5 cm. long
Number of flowers: 7–8

82. *Bulbophyllum secundum* Hk. f.

Thai name:–
Distribution: North, Upper Northeast, East
Flowering period: February–March
Characteristics: Dorsal sepal light green outside, blackish purple striped inside, lip blackish purple with ciliae.
Size: 0.7 cm., flowers closely spaced.
Number of flowers: Up to 15

83. *Bulbophyllum sessile* (Koen) J. J. Sm.

Thai name:–
Distribution: North, Northeast, East, South
Flowering period: May
Characteristics: Creamy white flower, sepals and petals long and narrow.
Size: 0.2 cm. wide and 0.5 cm. long
Number of flowers: 1

84. *Bulbophyllum siamense* Rchb. f.

Thai name:–
Distribution: North, Northeast, Central, East, West, South
Flowering period: May–July
Characteristics: Creamy yellow flower with dark brown veins, dorsal sepal more than 3 cm. long with no transversal bars between veins.
Size: 4.5 cm.
Number of flowers: 1

85. *Bulbophyllum suavissimum* Rolfe.

Thai name:–
Distribution: North, Lower Northeast, West
Flowering period: January
Characteristics: Yellow sepals and petals with strong yellow lip.
Size: 0.8 cm.
Number of flowers: 15-cm.-long inflorecence
Scent: Coumarin-scented

86. *Bulbophyllum tortuosum* (Bl.) Lindl.

Thai name:–
Distribution: South
Flowering period: June–July
Characteristics: Reddish flower, lip and sepals short, hairy at edges.
Size: 0.2 cm. wide and 0.3–0.4 cm. long
Number of flowers: 1

87. *Bulbophyllum tridentatum* Krzl.

Thai name:–
Distribution: East
Flowering period: February
Characteristics: Light brown sepals and petals with reddish lines, lip reddish brown.
Size: 0.6 cm. wide and 1 cm. long
Number of flowers: 6–7-cm.-long inflorescence

88. *Bulbophyllum tripaleum* Seidenf.

Thai name:–
Distribution: North
Flowering period: January–February
Characteristics: Sepals and petals light green, palea transversely banded red and white.
Size: 0.3 cm. wide and 0.8 cm. long
Number of flowers: 1 cm. dense head

89. *Bulbophyllum tripudians* Par. & Rchb. f.

Thai name: Tri Phut
ตรีภูติ
Distribution: North
Flowering period: January–April
Characteristics: Brownish orange flower with white lip.
Size: 0.7 cm. wide and 3.8 cm. long
Number of flowers: Up to 20

90. *Bulbophyllum triste* Rchb. f.

Thai name:–
Distribution: North, West
Flowering period: December–April
Characteristics: Purplish flowers, lip reddish purple.
Size: 0.3 cm. wide and 1 cm. long
Number of flowers: 3.5-cm.-long inflorescence

91. *Bulbophyllum umbellata* Lindl.

Thai name:–
Distribution: North
Flowering period: June
Characteristics: Light greenish sepals and petals with purple longitudinal lines, lip light pink.
Size: 1.2 cm.
Number of flowers: 4 umbellated flowers

92. *Bulbophyllum wallichii* Rchb. f.

Thai name:–
Distribution: North, Upper Northeast
Flowering period: January
Characteristics: Orange-yellow lateral sepals with very fine lines, inner surface of dorsal sepals ciliated at edges, lip reddish purple.
Size: 0.5 cm. wide and 3.5 cm. long
Number of flowers: 10

93. *Bulbophyllum wendlandianum* (Krzl.) Dammer

Thai name: Singto Lep Yieo
สิงโตเล็บเหยี่ยว
Distribution: North
Flowering period: May–July
Characteristics: Pinkish flower with purple lines on the petals, petals with palea at apex.
Size: 0.6 cm. wide and 9 cm. long
Number of flowers: 4–7

94. *Calanthe cardioglossa* Schltr.

Thai name: Uang Liam, Uang Nam Ton
เอื้องเหลี่ยม, เอื้องน้ำต้น

Distribution: North, Northeast, East, South

Flowering period: November–February

Characteristics: White to light lavender to deep rose flowers which change to orange or yellow before dropping, sidelobes of lip has dark purple blotches and stripes, lip trilobed.

Size: 1.2–1.5 cm. across, two flowers open at a time.

Number of flowers: 10–15

95. *Calanthe lyroglossa* Rchb. f.

Thai name:–

Distribution: Northeast, South

Flowering period: November–December

Characteristics: Yellow flowers, lip with very small sidelobes, operculum purplish brown.

Size: 1 cm.

Number of flowers: 25 or more

96. *Calanthe masuca* (D. Don) Lindl.

Thai name:–
Distribution: North, Upper Northeast, South
Flowering period: July
Characteristics: Light mauve flower with purple lip, midlobe of lip fan-shaped and emarginated at apex.
Size: 2.5–3 cm.
Number of flowers: 10–15

97. *Calanthe rosea* (Lindl.) Benth.

Thai name:–
Distribution: North, Upper Northeast, West
Flowering period: November
Characteristics: Rosy pink flower with white throat, lip square.
Size: 4.5 cm. across
Number of flowers: Up to 20

98. *Calanthe rubens* Ridley

Thai name:–
Distribution: Lower Northeast, Central, East, South
Flowering period: December
Characteristics: Pink flower with dark red lip base and column.
Size: 3 cm.
Number of flowers: 15

99. *Calanthe triplicata* (Willem.) Ames

Thai name: Uang Khao Tok
เอื้องข้าวตอก
Distribution: North, Northeast, East, West, South
Flowering period: June
Characteristics: White flower with green tip, four-lobed white lip with three orange keels at base.
Size: 2 cm.
Number of flowers: 50 flowers dense to 10-cm.-wide inflorescence

100. *Calanthe vestita* Lindl.

Thai name: Khao Malila
ขาวมะลิลา
Distribution: Northeast, West, South
Flowering period: October–February
Characteristics: White flower, trilobed white lip with yellow marking in the throat.
Size: 5 cm. wide and 6 cm. long
Number of flowers: Up to 15

101. *Cheirostylis thailandica* Seidenf.

Thai name:–
Distribution: North, West
Flowering period: June
Characteristics: Brownish flower with white lip and two green patches at epichile base.
Size: 0.7 cm. wide and 1 cm. long
Number of flowers: 5–7

102. *Chilochista exuperei* (Guill.) Garay

Thai name: Phaya Rai Bai
พญาไร้ใบ
Distribution: North, Northeast
Flowering period: September–October
Characteristics: White flowers, sidelobes of lip inside with dark brownish purple lines.
Size: 0.8 cm.
Number of flowers: 5–10

103. *Chilochista lunifera* (Rchb. f.) J. J. Sm.

Thai name: Phaya Rai Bai
พญาไร้ใบ
Distribution: North
Flowering period: March–April
Characteristics: Sepals and petals brownish red with yellow edges, sidelobes of lip white, midlobes white with two brownish red dots.
Size: 0.8 cm.
Number of flowers: 10–20

104. *Chilochista parishii* Seidenf.

Thai name: Phaya Rai Bai
พญาไร้ใบ

Distribution: North, Northeast, Central, West, South

Flowering period: March–April

Characteristics: Light greenish yellow flowers with numerous brown spots, lip white, sidelobes of lip with distal brown blotches.

Size: 1.2 cm.

Number of flowers: Up to 15

105. *Chilochista viridiflava* Seidenf.

Thai name: Phaya Rai Bai
พญาไร้ใบ

Distribution: North

Flowering period: April–June

Characteristics: Greenish yellow flowers, lip white with few light red-brown blotches on sack and inside of sidelobes.

Size: 1.2 cm.

Number of flowers: Up to 20

106. *Cirrhopetalum concinnum* Hook f.

Thai name: Singto Bai Phat Daeng
สิงโตใบพัดแดง
Distribution: South
Flowering period: October–November
Characteristics: Ruby red flowers, lip purple with yellow tip.
Size: 0.3 cm. wide and 1.5 cm. long
Number of flowers: 6–7

107. *Cirrhopetalum dentiferum* (Ridl.) Garay, Hamer & Siegerist

Thai name:–
Distribution: South
Flowering period: April
Characteristics: Light lilac petals and sepals with violet dots, lip light purple.
Size: 0.6 cm. wide and 1.3 cm. long
Number of flowers: 6–8

108. *Cirrhopetalum lepidum* (Bl.) Schltr.

Thai name: Singto Bai Phat Daeng
สิงโตใบพัดแดง
Distribution: North, Northeast, East, South
Flowering period: August–December
Characteristics: Dorsal sepal yellow, edges purple hairy, lateral sepals cream suffused with rosy mauve towards the base, lip brown.
Size: 0.7 cm. wide and 2 cm. long
Number of flowers: 5–10

109. *Cirrhopetalum picturatum* Lodd. ex Lindl.

Thai name: Phat Luang
พัดเหลือง
Distribution: North
Flowering period: October–January
Characteristics: Greenish yellow flowers, dorsal sepal with purplish red spots at tip, petals and base of sepals likewise.
Size: 0.5 cm. wide and 3 cm. long
Number of flowers: 7–9

110. *Cleisomeria lanatum* Lindl.

Thai name: Kho Kwang
คอกว่าง
Distribution: North, Upper Northeast, East, West, South
Flowering period: June–August
Characteristics: Chartreuse sepals and petals with three reddish brown lines, lip white with purple tip, apex of lip with two horns.
Size: 0.5 cm.
Number of flowers: 9-cm.-long inflorescence

111. *Cleisomeria pilosulum* (Gagnep.) Seidenf. & Garay

Thai name:–
Distribution: North, Northeast, East, West
Flowering period: June–August
Characteristics: Greenish white sepals and petals, lateral sepals with brownish median lines, lip light pink.
Size: 0.5 cm.
Number of flowers: 9-cm.-long branched inflorescence

112. *Cleisostoma arietinum* (Rchb. f.) Garay

Thai name: Khao Phae
เขาแพะ
Distribution: North, Northeast, South, West
Flowering period: October–March
Characteristics: Light purple flower, sidelobes of lip erect, triangular with dark purple tips.
Size: 0.5 cm.
Number of flowers: 20–40

113. *Cleisostoma chantaburiense* Seidenf.

Thai name: Kang Pla Muang Chan
ก้างปลาเมืองจันท์
Distribution: Lower Northeast, Central
Flowering period: August
Characteristics: Yellow sepals and petals with three brownish red streaks on each, lip cream with red basal patch.
Size: 1.2 cm.
Number of flowers: 5–7

114. *Cleisostoma crochetii* (Guill.) Garay

Thai name:–
Distribution: North, Upper Northeast, East
Flowering period: August
Characteristics: Sepals and petals white with purple tinted, midlobe of lip purple with white tip, sidelobes and midlobe raising vertically as three horns.
Size: 0.7 cm.
Number of flowers: 10–18-cm.-long inflorescence

115. *Cleisostoma discolor* Lindl.

Thai name:–
Distribution: Northeast, Central, East, South
Flowering period: May
Characteristics: Greenish yellow sepals and petals with dark brown median lines, lip creamy white with purple markings.
Size: 1 cm.
Number of flowers: 20

116. *Cleisostoma duplicilobum* (J. J. Sm.) Garay

Thai name:–
Distribution: North, Lower Northeast, East, West
Flowering period: May
Characteristics: Light green sepals and petals with two reddish brown stripes, lip cream.
Size: 0.8 cm.
Number of flowers: 25

117. *Cleisostoma elegans* Seidenf.

Thai name:–

Distribution: North, Northeast, West, South

Flowering period: August–September

Characteristics: Light yellow flowers with purple lip, midlobe of lip upward and inward curved.

Size: 0.7 cm.

Number of flowers: 20-cm.-long inflorescence

118. *Cleisostoma filiforme* (Lindl.) Garay

Thai name:–

Distribution: North, Upper Northeast

Flowering period: July

Characteristics: Sepals and petals light green with brownish purple spots, midlobe of lip lilac.

Size: 0.6 cm.

Number of flowers: 30

119. *Cleisostoma fuerstenbergianum* Krzl.

Thai name: Kang Pla
ก้างปลา

Distribution: North, Upper Northeast, East, West, South

Flowering period: August–September

Characteristics: Dark brown flowers with white lips that turn to yellow with age, midlobe upward pointing.

Size: 1 cm.

Number of flowers: 15–18-cm.-long inflorescence

120. *Cleisostoma linearilobatum* (Seidenf. & Smitin.) Garay

Thai name:–
Distribution: North, Upper Northeast
Flowering period: June
Characteristics: Dorsal sepal and petals dark brown with a green median line, lateral sepal distal half dark brown, proximal half green, spur light purple.
Size: 0.6 cm.
Number of flowers: 30

121. *Cleisostoma paniculatum* (Ker-Gawl.) Garay

Thai name:–
Distribution: Upper Northeast, Central
Flowering period: June
Characteristics: Sepals and petals yellowish green with brown lines, lip yellow with brownish tint at tip of sidelobes.
Size: 0.7 cm.
Number of flowers: 10–15 per branch

122. *Cleisostome racemiferum* (Lindl.) Garay

Thai name: Uang Cho Ma Muang
เอื้องช่อมะม่วง
Distribution: North, East, West
Flowering period: June
Characteristics: Sepals and petals light yellow with two dark red brown patches, sack white.
Size: 0.9 cm.
Number of flowers: 30 per branch

123. *Cleisostoma rolfeanum* (King & Plantl.) Garay

Thai name:–
Distribution: North
Flowering period: August
Characteristics: Light green sepals and petals with brown stripes, median line light yellow, midlobe of lip light purple with lighter tip, sidelobes very light purple.
Size: 0.8 cm
Number of flowers: 20

124. *Cleisostoma rostratum* (Lindl.) Garay

Thai name:–
Distribution: Upper Northeast
Flowering period: July
Characteristics: Yellowish green sepals and petals with two brown patches, lip and sack purple.
Size: 0.8 cm.
Number of flowers: 35–45

125. *Cleisostoma simondii* (Gagnep.) Seidenf.

Thai name:–
Distribution: North, Upper Northeast, West, South
Flowering period: October–November
Characteristics: Brownish yellow flower, with midlobe near to white apex.
Size: 1.5 cm.
Number of flowers: Up to 15

126. *Cleisostoma subulatum* Bl.

Thai name:–
Distribution: North, Northeast, East, West, South
Flowering period: August
Characteristics: Light green sepals and petals with two brown patches, lip and sack white.
Size: 0.8 cm.
Number of flowers: 45–50

127. *Cleisostoma tenuifolium* (L.) Garay

Thai name:–
Distribution: South
Flowering period: December
Characteristics: Yellow sepals and petals with brown streaks on the upper half, lip white with two tiny spots on tips of sidelobes.
Size: 0.4 cm.
Number of flowers: 12

128. *Cleisostoma williamsonii* (Rchb. f.) Garay

Thai name:–
Distribution: North, South
Flowering period: September
Characteristics: Dark brown sepals and petals, sidelobes of lip white, midlobe of lip purple with white apex.
Size: 0.7 cm.
Number of flowers: 12–15-cm.-long inflorescence

129. *Coelogyne assamica* Linden & Rchb. f.

Thai name:–
Distribution: Lower Northeast
Flowering period: September
Characteristics: Light yellow sepals and petals, lip white with three brown lines in the center, sidelobes with brown tints and spots.
Size: 3.5 cm. wide and 5 cm. long
Number of flowers: 2–3

130. *Coelogyne brachyptera* Rchb. f.

Thai name:–
Distribution: North, Northeast, East
Flowering period: March–April
Characteristics: Light green flower with black blotches and spots on lighter green midlobe.
Size: 5 cm. across
Number of flowers: 3–5

131. *Coelogyne cumingii* Lindl.

Thai name:–
Distribution: North, Lower Northeast, East, South
Flowering period: April
Characteristics: White flower with three finely waved yellow keels on the white lip.
Size: 3.5 cm.
Number of flowers: 10

132. *Coelogyne flavida* Wall. ex Lindl.

Thai name:–
Distribution: North, Upper Northeast
Flowering period: February
Characteristics: Light yellow flower with two brown keels on the lip.
Size: 1.7–2 cm.
Number of flowers: 5–6

133. *Coelogyne fimbriata* Lindl.

Thai name:–
Distribution: North, Lower Northeast
Flowering period: October
Characteristics: Pale greenish yellow sepals and petals, sidelobes of lip with brownish purple lines, edges of midlobe fringed with two dark brown keels on the lip.
Size: 3.5 cm.
Number of flowers: 2

134. *Coelogyne fuscescens* var. *brunnea* (Lindl.) Lindl.

Thai name:–
Distribution: North, Upper Northeast
Flowering period: December
Characteristics: Light yellow flower, lip with golden brown edges on sidelobes and base of epichile.
Size: 5 cm.
Number of flowers: 1–2

135. *Coelogyne lactea* Rchb. f.

Thai name: Uang Hin
เอื้องหิน
Distribution: North, Upper Northeast
Flowering period: February–May
Characteristics: White flower with three keels ending at base of epichile.
Size: 4.5 cm.
Number of flowers: Up to 10

136. *Coelogyne lentiginosa* Lindl.

Thai name: Uang Chun
เอื้องฉุน
Distribution: North, Upper Northeast, West, South
Flowering period: September–December
Characteristics: Light greenish yellow sepals and petals, lip white with dark brown edge of sidelobes and yellowish brown at base of midlobe.
Size: 4 cm.
Number of flowers: 4–5

137. *Coelogyne nitida* Lindl.

Thai name:–
Distribution: North
Flowering period: May
Characteristics: White flower with beautiful yellow markings on lip.
Size: 4 cm.
Number of flowers: 5–7

138. *Coelogyne ovalis* Lindl.

Thai name:–
Distribution: North, Lower Northeast
Flowering period: January
Characteristics: Light yellowish green flower, lip fringed with two brown keels from base but not reaching apex.
Size: 4 cm.
Number of flowers: 1–2

139. *Coelogyne pallens* Ridl.

Thai name:–
Distribution: East
Flowering period: November
Characteristics: Light yellow flower, lip cream with brown sidelobes, midlobe with one low median and two long high and wavy keels, edges of lip ciliated.
Size: 2.5 cm.
Number of flowers: 2–3

140. *Coelogyne tenasserimensis* Seidenf.

Thai name:–
Distribution: North, West
Flowering period: February
Characteristics: Yellow sepals and petals, two long keels and base of lip dark brown.
Size: 2 cm.
Number of flowers: 4

141. *Coelogyne trinervis* Lindl.

Thai name: Uang Mak
เอื้องหมาก
Distribution: North, Northeast, East, West, South
Flowering period: November
Characteristics: Creamy white sepals and petals, lip cream with brown lines on midlobe, sidelobes brown inside and outside.
Size: 4 cm.
Number of flowers: 5–6

142. *Coelogyne viscosa* Rchb. f.

Thai name: Uang Sam Dok
เอื้องสามดอก
Distribution: North, Northeast, East, West
Flowering period: January
Characteristics: White sepals and petals, lip bright yellow with three wavy keels ended at epichile base, sidelobes of lip with brown stripes.
Size: 4 cm.
Number of flowers: 3

143. *Cryptopylos clausus* (J. J. Sm.) Garay

Thai name:–
Distribution: Northeast
Flowering period: June
Characteristics: Greenish yellow sepals and petals with brown markings, lip light green, operculum purple.
Size: 2 cm.
Number of flowers: 12

144. *Cymbidium aloifolium* (L.) Sw.

Thai name: Ka Re Ka Ron
กะเรกะร่อน
Distribution: North, Northeast, East, South
Flowering period: March–May
Characteristics: Reddish brown sepals and petals bordered by white, lip with red-purple stripes, anther cap yellow. Pure yellow flower is quite rare.
Size: 4 cm.
Number of flowers: Up to 30

145. *Cymbidium ensifolium* (L.) Sw.

Thai name: Chu Lan
จุหลัน
Distribution: North, Upper Northeast, South
Flowering period: November–January
Characteristics: Greenish based flowers striped with reddish brown, lip light yellow with many reddish brown streaks, anther cap yellow.
Size: 6.5 cm.
Number of flowers: 15–18
Scent: Highly fragrant

146. *Cymbidium findlaysonianum* Lindl.

Thai name: Ka Re Ka Ron Pak Pet
กะเรกะร่อนปากเป็ด
Distribution: Upper Northeast, Central, East, South
Flowering period: May
Characteristics: Sepals, petals and column dirty yellow to greenish cream flushed with purple, lip white, midlobe with a large deep pink crescent-shaped patch at tip.
Size: 4.5 cm.
Number of flowers: 15

147. *Cymbidium lancifolium* Hook

Thai name:–
Distribution: North, Northeast, East
Flowering period: May
Characteristics: Greenish white sepals and petals with purple median lines, lip white, midlobe with transversal purple markings.
Size: 3.5 cm.
Number of flowers: 5–6

148. *Cymbidium lowianum* Rchb. f.

Thai name: Ka Re Ka Ron Doi
กะเรกะร่อนดอย
Distribution: North
Flowering period: November–January
Characteristics: Sepals and petals greenish yellow with faint reddish brown streaks, lip creamy white with deep maroon patch.
Size: 10 cm.
Number of flowers: Up to 20

149. *Cymbidium siamense* Rolfe ex Downie

Thai name:–
Distribution: North, Northeast, Central
Flowering period: January
Characteristics: Sepals and petals yellowish green with red longitudinal lines, lip pale greenish yellow with red transversal blotches.
Size: 4 cm.
Number of flowers: 5–6

150. *Cymbidium sinense* (Jacks. in Andr.) Willd.

Thai name:–
Distribution: North, Northeast
Flowering period: August
Characteristics: Sepals and petals chartreuse with reddish brown stripes, midlobe creamy white with reddish brown streaks.
Size: 3.7 cm.
Number of flowers: 6 or more

151. *Cymbidium tracyanum* L. Castle

Thai name: Uang Kamboe, Ka Re Ka Ron Inthanon
เอื้องกำเบ้อ, กะเรกะร่อนอินทนนท์
Distribution: North, Upper Northeast
Flowering period: October–January
Characteristics: Greenish yellow sepals and petals with reddish brown stripes, lip yellow with many short maroon streaks.
Size: 11–12 cm.
Number of flowers: 15–20
Scent: Highly fragrant

152. *Dendrobium aciculare* Lindl.

Thai name:–
Distribution: East, South
Flowering period: August
Characteristics: Sepals and petals greenish yellow, lip white, sidelobes inside with purple veins, keels yellow, reddish at apex, epichile of lip fringed.
Size: 1 cm.
Number of flowers: 1

153. *Dendrobium acinaciforme* Roxb.

Thai name: Uang Takhap
เอื้องตะขาบ
Distribution: North, Northeast, East, South
Flowering period: August
Characteristics: White sepals and petals, white lip with yellow patch on the center.
Size: 1 cm.
Number of flowers: 1

154. *Dendrobium albosanguineum* Lindl.

Thai name: Uang Pha Wiang
เอื้องผาเวียง
Distribution: North
Flowering period: February–March
Characteristics: Creamy white petals and sepals with two dark maroon blotches at lip base.
Size: 6.5 cm.
Number of flowers: 1–2

155. *Dendrobium aloifolium* (Bl.) Rchb. f.

Thai name: Uang Mani, Uang Chang
เอื้องมณี, เอื้องช้าง
Distribution: North, East, West, South
Flowering period: July
Characteristics: Pure white sepals and petals which are much recurved, lip white and bilobed.
Size: 0.4 cm.
Number of flowers: 1

156. *Dendrobium alterum* Seidenf.

Thai name: Uang Khem
เอื้องเข็ม
Distribution: North, Northeast
Flowering period: June
Characteristics: Sepals and petals light yellow with longitudinal dots along veins, lip orange yellow with light purple flush.
Size: 1 cm.
Number of flowers: 2–5 flowers per node

157. *Dendrobium anosmum* Lindl.

Thai name: Uang Sai Luang
เอื้องสายหลวง
Distribution: Northeast, South
Flowering period: February–April
Characteristics: Sepals and petals rosy purple with two deep purple blotches in the convoluted and finely pubescent lip.
Size: 6.5–7 cm.
Number of flowers: 1 flower per node

158. *Dendrobium aphyllum* (Roxb.) C. E. C. Fisher

Thai name: Uang Sai Long Laeng
เอื้องสายล่องแล่ง
Distribution: Widely distributed
Flowering period: March–April
Characteristics: Very light mauve sepals and petals, petals broader than dorsal sepal, lip pale yellow with purple veins to the base.
Size: 5 cm.
Number of flowers: 1–4 flowers per node

159. *Dendrobium bellatulum* Rolfe.

Thai name: Uang Sae Mon
เอื้องแซะหม่น
Distribution: North, Upper Northeast
Flowering period: January–March
Characteristics: Creamy white flowers with cadmium orange lip, throat orange red.
Size: 3.8 cm.
Number of flowers: 1–2

160. *Dendrobium bilobulatum* Seidenf.

Thai name:–
Distribution: West, South
Flowering period: January
Characteristics: Flowers creamy white with fine purple lines on sepals and petals, epichile of lip bilobed by a deep split, center of lip with brownish orange warts.
Size: 1 cm.
Number of flowers: 3–4

161. *Dendrobium brymerianum* Rchb. f.

Thai name: Uang Kham Foi Pai
เอื้องคำฝอยปาย
Distribution: North, Upper Northeast
Flowering period: August
Characteristics: Golden flowers with long dented and fimbriated lip.
Size: 4.5 cm.
Number of flowers: 1–2

162. *Dendrobium capillipes* Rchb. f.

Thai name: Uang Kham Pok
เอื้องคำป๊อก
Distribution: North, Upper Northeast, West, South
Flowering period: February–April
Characteristics: Bright yellow flowers on 2–3-cm. pseudobulb, lip much longer than sepals and petals.
Size: 3 cm.
Number of flowers: 3–5

163. *Dendrobium cariniferum* Rchb. f.

Thai name: Uang Ngoen Daeng
เอื้องเงินแดง
Distribution: North
Flowering period: February–April
Characteristics: Sepals and petals creamy white with yellow tips, midlobe of lip creamy yellow, sidelobes darker yellow, throat reddish orange and ciliated.
Size: 5 cm.
Number of flowers: 2–5

164. *Dendrobium chittimae* Seidenf.

Thai name:–
Distribution: Northeast
Flowering period: February
Characteristics: Creamy white sepals and petals, center of lip with greenish yellow tufted area, sidelobes with fine purple lines.
Size: 2.5 cm.
Number of flowers: 1

165. *Dendrobium christyanum* Rchb. f.

Thai name: Uang Sae Doi Pui
เอื้องแซะดอยปุย
Distribution: North, Upper Northeast
Flowering period: June–August
Characteristics: Creamy white sepals and petals, midlobe of lip white with yellow to red center.
Size: 3 cm.
Number of flowers: 1–2

166. *Dendrobium chrysanthum* Lindl.

Thai name: Uang Sai Morakot
เอื้องสายมรกต
Distribution: North, Upper Northeast
Flowering period: May–June
Characteristics: Bright golden yellow with two reddish brown blotches on the lip.
Size: 3.7–5 cm.
Number of flowers: 2–3 flowers per node

167. *Dendrobium chryseum* Rolfe

Thai name:–
Distribution: Upper Northeast
Flowering period: April
Characteristics: Golden flower with deep maroon blotch at base of fringed lip.
Size: 2.5 cm.
Number of flowers: 3–6

168. *Dendrobium chrysotoxum* Lindl.

Thai name: Uang Kham
เอื้องคำ
Distribution: North, Upper Northeast, West
Flowering period: February–May
Characteristics: Bright yellow sepals and petals, lip yellow-orange.
Size: 3.7 cm.
Number of flowers: 20 or more

169. *Dendrobium compactum* Rolfe ex W. Hackett

Thai name: Uang Khao Tok
เอื้องข้าวตอก
Distribution: North, Upper Northeast, West
Flowering period: October–November
Characteristics: White sepals and petals with greenish yellow fringed lip.
Size: 0.7 cm.
Number of flowers: 4–6

170. *Dendrobium crepidatum* Lindl.

Thai name: Uang Sai Nam Khieo
เอื้องสายน้ำเขียว
Distribution: North, Upper Northeast, Central, West
Flowering period: April
Characteristics: White sepals and petals tinged with lavender, white lip with yellow center.
Size: 3.7 cm.
Number of flowers: 2–3
Scent: Delicately fragrant

171. *Dendrobium cruentum* Rchb. f.

Thai name: Uang Nok Kaeo
เอื้องนกแก้ว
Distribution: South
Flowering period: Year round
Characteristics: Light green sepals and petals with dark green veins, lip creamy white flushed with red.
Size: 3.7–5 cm.
Number of flowers: 1–2

172. *Dendrobium crumenatum* Sw.

Thai name: Uang Mali, Wai Tamoi
เอื้องมะลิ, หวายตะมอย
Distribution: Lower Northeast, Central, West, East, South
Flowering period: March–July
Characteristics: Pure white sepals and petals, lip white with yellow patch.
Size: 4 cm.
Number of flowers: Up to 10
Scent: Fragrant

173. *Dendrobium crystallinum* Rchb. f.

Thai name: Uang Sai Sam Si
เอื้องสายสามสี
Distribution: North, Northeast, East, West
Flowering period: April–July
Characteristics: White sepals and petals with lavender to purple tips, white lip with yellow base and purple tip.
Size: 5–6 cm.
Number of flowers: 2–3 flowers at a node

174. *Dendrobium cumulatum* Lindl.

Thai name: Uang Sai Si Dok
เอื้องสายสี่ดอก
Distribution: North, East, South
Flowering period: July
Characteristics: Light rosy-purple flower, lip creamy white.
Size: 3 cm.
Number of flowers: 4–8

175. *Dendrobium delacourii* Guill.

Thai name: Uang Dok Ma Kham
เอื้องดอกมะขาม
Distribution: Widely distributed, except Central and South Thailand
Flowering period: April–May
Characteristics: Light greenish yellow sepals and petals, lip brownish yellow with brown stripes, sidelobes dark brown.
Size: 2 cm.
Number of flowers: 8–10

176. *Dendrobium densiflorum* Lindl.

Thai name: Uang Mon Khai Liam,
Uang Mon Khai Luang
เอื้องมอนไข่เหลี่ยม, เอื้องมอนไข่เหลือง
Distribution: North, Upper Northeast
Flowering period: August–September
Characteristics: Sepals and petals yellow, lip orange yellow. Inflorescence dense.
Size: 3 cm.
Number of flowers: Up to 50

177. *Dendrobium devonianum* Paxt.

Thai name: Uang Sai Man Phra In,
Uang Sai Luat
เอื้องสายม่านพระอินทร์, เอื้องสายลวด
Distribution: North, Upper Northeast
Flowering period: May–August
Characteristics: White sepals and petals with purple tips, lip white with two golden blotches toward the base, tip dark purple.
Size: 2.5 cm.
Number of flowers: 6–7

178. *Dendrobium dixanthum* Rchb. f.

Thai name: Uang Kham Pon, Uang Bai Phai
เอื้องคำปอน, เอื้องใบไผ่

Distribution: North, Upper Northeast, East, West

Flowering period: February–March

Characteristics: Bright buttercup yellow with golden lip, petal margins very finely dentate.

Size: 3 cm.

Number of flowers: Up to 5 flowers at each node

179. *Dendrobium dixonianum* Rolfe ex Downie

Thai name:–

Distribution: North

Flowering period: October

Characteristics: Greenish white flower, lip greenish yellow with three dark lines.

Size: 1 cm.

Number of flowers: 3–5

180. *Dendrobium draconis* Rchb. f.

Thai name: Uang Ngoen
เอื้องเงิน

Distribution: North, Northeast, East, West

Flowering period: March–April

Characteristics: Pure white sepals and petals, lip white with orange–red lines toward the base.

Size: 6.5 cm.

Number of flowers: 2–5

181. *Dendrobium ellipsophyllum* Tang & Wang

Thai name: Uang Thong
เอื้องทอง
Distribution: North, Northeast, East, West, South
Flowering period: August–October
Characteristics: Fawn sepals and petals, lip orange yellow with three long dark brown lines.
Size: 1.2 cm.
Number of flowers: 1–2
Scent: Fragrant

182. *Dendrobium eriiflorum* Griff.

Thai name:–
Distribution: North
Flowering period: October
Characteristics: Light green flowers, lip serrated with green edge and green venation.
Size: 0.8 cm.
Number of flowers: 5–6

183. *Dendrobium exile* Schltr.

Thai name: Sae Phra–In
แส้พระอินทร์
Distribution: North, West
Flowering period: December
Characteristics: Pure white flower, lip inside with very minute red or orange dots, disc yellow.
Size: 2–2.5 cm.
Number of flowers: 1–2

184. *Dendrobium falconeri* Hook

Thai name: Uang Sai Wisut
เอื้องสายวิสูตร
Distribution: North
Flowering period: January–February
Characteristics: White sepals and petals with purple tips, lip white with purple tip and big dark maroon blotch in the throat bordered with yellow-orange patch.
Number of flowers: 1–2 flowers per node

185. *Dendrobium farmeri* Paxt.

Thai name: Uang Matchanu
เอื้องมัจฉาณุ
Distribution: North, East, West, South
Flowering period: February
Characteristics: White sepals and petals with violet tint, lip orange yellow with white apex. Lip blade not papillous.
Size: 2.5 cm.
Number of flowers: Up to 20

186. *Dendrobium fimbriatum* Hook

Thai name: Uang Waeo Mayura,
Uang Kham Ta Dam
เอื้องแววมยุรา, เอื้องคำตาดำ
Distribution: North, Upper Northeast, West
Flowering period: April–May
Characteristics: Golden sepals and petals with dark maroon blotch at the base of the fimbriated lip.
Size: 3–3.7 cm.
Number of flowers: 6–12

187. *Dendrobium findlayanum* Par. & Rchb. f.

Thai name: Uang Phuang Yok, Wai Pom
เอื้องพวงหยก, หวายปม
Distribution: North
Flowering period: February–March
Characteristics: Pale lavender sepals and petals, lip center saffron yellow, upper side of lip finely pubescent.
Size: 4.3–5 cm.
Number of flowers: 2–3 flowers per node

188. *Dendrobium formosum* Roxb. ex Lindl.

Thai name: Uang Ngoen Luang
เอื้องเงินหลวง
Distribution: North, Upper Northeast, West, South
Flowering period: October–December
Characteristics: White sepals and petals, white lip with yellow blotch.
Size: 10 cm.
Number of flowers: 2–4
Scent: Delicately fragrant

189. *Dendrobium friedericksianum* Rchb.f.

Thai name: Wai Luang Chantabun, Luang Nok Khamin
หวายเหลืองจันทบูร, เหลืองนกขมิ้น
Distribution: Lower Northeast, East
Flowering period: January–March
Characteristics: Chrome yellow sepals and petals with or without blotches at the throat of the darker yellow lip.
Size: 5.5 cm.
Number of flowers: 2–4

190. *Dendrobium gibsonii* Lindl.

Thai name: Uang Kham Ta
เอื้องคำตา
Distribution: North
Flowering period: April
Characteristics: Sepals and petals bright yellow, lip also bright yellow with two dark maroon blotches.
Size: 2.5–3.5 cm.
Number of flowers: Up to 10

191. *Dendrobium gratiotissimum* Rchb. f.

Thai name: King Dam
กิ่งดำ
Distribution: North
Flowering period: February
Characteristics: White sepals and petals with lavender tips, lip has bright yellow center with lavender tip.
Size: 3.7 cm.
Number of flowers: 2–3 flowers per node

192. *Dendrobium gregulus* Seidenf.

Thai name:–
Distribution: North, West
Flowering period: February
Characteristics: Light brownish yellow flower, lip with many brownish purple lines.
Size: 1 cm.
Number of flowers: 5–6

193. *Dendrobium griffithianum* Lindl.

Thai name: Uang Matcha Luang
เอื้องมัจฉาเหลือง
Distribution: North, Upper Northeast, West, South
Flowering period: July–September
Characteristics: Sepals and petals amber-yellow, lip cadmium orange. Inflorescence not so dense.
Size: 3.3 cm.
Number of flowers: Up to 30

194. *Dendrobium harveyanum* Rchb. f.

Thai name: Uang Kham Foi
เอื้องคำฝอย
Distribution: North
Flowering period: April–May
Characteristics: Bright canary yellow sepals and petals, edges of petals and lip deeply ciliated.
Size: 3 cm.
Number of flowers: 3–4

195. *Dendrobium hendersonii* Hawkes & Heller

Thai name:–
Distribution: West, South
Flowering period: June
Characteristics: Pinkish cream sepals and petals with pink color on their backs, lip has reddish lines with yellow callus on the center.
Size: 2.2 cm.
Number of flowers: 1

196. *Dendrobium hercoglossum* Rchb. f.

Thai name: Uang Dok Makhua
เอื้องดอกมะเขือ
Distribution: East
Flowering period: February–April
Characteristics: Light mauve sepals and petals, hollow white lip with dark purple anther.
Size: 2.5 cm.
Number of flowers: 4–5 flowers per node

197. *Dendrobium heterocarpum* Lindl.

Thai name: Uang Si Tan
เอื้องสีตาล
Distribution: North, Northeast, West
Flowering period: December–February
Characteristics: Creamy yellow sepals and petals, lip darker yellow with reddish brown veins.
Size: 5–6 cm.
Number of flowers: 2–3 flowers per node
Scent: Fragrant

198. *Dendrobium indivisum* (Bl.) Miq.

Thai name:–
Distribution: North, Upper Northeast
Flowering period: July
Characteristics: Greenish yellow flower with purple stripes and markings, lip without distinct sidelobes.
Size: 0.8 cm.
Number of flowers: 1–2

199. *Dendrobium indivisum* var. *lampangense* Rolfe

Thai name:–
Distribution: North, Upper Northeast
Flowering period: May
Characteristics: Light greenish yellow flower, lip with distinct sidelobes and purple stripes.
Size: 0.7 cm.
Number of flowers: 1–2

200. *Dendrobium indivisum* var. *pallidum* Seidenf.

Thai name:–
Distribution: East, South
Flowering period: August–September
Characteristics: Greenish yellow flower with no stripe, lip recurved.
Size: 0.7 cm.
Number of flowers: 1

201. *Dendrobium infundibulum* Lindl.

Thai name: Uang Ta Hoen
เอื้องตาเหิน
Distribution: North, Upper Northeast, West
Flowering period: February–March
Characteristics: White flower, white lip with cadmium orange blotch, epichile with a rather deep V-shaped sinus at apex.
Size: 8 cm.
Number of flowers: 2–3

202. *Dendrobium jenkensii* Wall. ex Lindl.

Thai name: Uang Phung Noi
เอื้องผึ้งน้อย
Distribution: North, Upper Northeast
Flowering period: March
Characteristics: Golden flower with darker color on the pubescent lip.
Size: 2.5 cm.
Number of flowers: 1–3

203. *Dendrobium keithii* Ridl.

Thai name:–
Distribution: Lower Northeast, East, South
Flowering period: May–July
Characteristics: Greenish yellow sepals and petals, hypochile with convex red edges, epichile with a deep split separated in two overlapping lobules.
Size: 1.1 cm.
Number of flowers: 1

204. *Dendrobium kentrophyllum* Hk. f.

Thai name:–
Distribution: East, South
Flowering period: November
Characteristics: Pure white flower, lip with a median yellow band.
Size: 1.7 cm.
Number of flowers: 1

205. *Dendrobium kratense* Kerr

Thai name:–
Distribution: East, South
Flowering period: October
Characteristics: Sepals and petals white, lip greenish white with grass green veins.
Size: 1 cm.
Number of flowers: 4 per branch

206. *Dendrobium lamellatum* (Bl.) Lindl.

Thai name:–
Distribution: South
Flowering period: March
Characteristics: White flower with a green or dirty orange center, lip fan-shaped with recurved epichile.
Size: 1.7 cm.
Number of flowers: 3–4

207. *Dendrobium leonis* (Lindl.) Rchb. f.

Thai name: Uang Takhap Yai
เอื้องตะขาบใหญ่
Distribution: North, Lower Northeast, East, South
Flowering period: Year round
Characteristics: Yellow to greenish yellow flower, often with purple markings, lip apex notched.
Size: 1 cm.
Number of flowers: 1

208. *Dendrobium lindleyi* Steud.

Thai name: Uang Phung
เอื้องผึ้ง
Distribution: North, Upper Northeast, East, West, South
Flowering period: March–May
Characteristics: Pale to bright yellow flower, lip base golden yellow and pubescent bordered with paler yellow.
Size: 3 cm.
Number of flowers: Up to 20

209. *Dendrobium linguella* Rchb. f.

Thai name:–
Distribution: South
Flowering period: March
Characteristics: Pale mauve flowers with dark purple operculum.
Size: 1.7 cm.
Number of flowers: 4–5 per node

210. *Dendrobium lituiflorum* Lindl.

Thai name: Uang Khrang Sai Yao
เอื้องครั่งสายยาว
Distribution: North, Upper Northeast
Flowering period: February–March
Characteristics: Sepals purple, petals darker, lip white, cornet–shaped with purple center surrounded by white band and purple margin.
Size: 5 cm.
Number of flowers: 1–2 flowers per node

211. *Dendrobium mannii* Ridl.

Thai name: Uang Hang Pla
เอื้องหางปลา
Distribution: North, Upper Northeast, East, West, South
Flowering period: March
Characteristics: Pinkish brown flower, lip with small warts, epichile of lip bilobulated. Flowers are along stem after shedding of all leaves.
Size: 1 cm.
Number of flowers: 1

212. *Dendrobium monticola* Hunt & Summerh.

Thai name:–
Distribution: North
Flowering period: November
Characteristics: Flowers greenish white, sidelobes with brownish veins, edges of hypochile inciso-surrulate.
Size: 1.5 cm.
Number of flowers: 2–3

213. *Dendrobium moschatum* (Buch.-Ham.) Sw.

Thai name: Uang Champa
เอื้องจำปา
Distribution: North, Upper Northeast, East, West, South
Flowering period: March–May
Characteristics: Sepals and petals orange-yellow with two maroon blotches in the cupped lip.
Size: 7.5–10 cm.
Number of flowers: 8–15

214. *Dendrobium nathanielis* Rchb. f.

Thai name: Klet Nim
เกล็ดนิ่ม
Distribution: Upper Northeast, East, West, South
Flowering period: March
Characteristics: Pinkish yellow sepals and petals with purplish brown stripes, lip pale pink with small yellow warts, lip apex bilobed.
Size: 1 cm.
Number of flowers: 1–3

215. *Dendrobium nobile* Lindl.

Thai name: Uang Kao Kiu
เอื้องเก๊ากิ่ว
Distribution: North, Upper Northeast
Flowering period: March–April
Characteristics: Sepals and petals purple to white with purple tips, some have maroon blotch in the throat with yellow or white border and a pale lavender touch.
Size: 5.5 cm.
Number of flowers: 2–4 flowers per node

216. *Dendrobium ochreatum* Lindl.

Thai name: Uang Kham Phak Prap
เอื้องคำผักปราบ
Distribution: North, Upper Northeast
Flowering period: June
Characteristics: Bright yellow sepals and petals, lip golden yellow with dark maroon central blotches.
Size: 4 cm.
Number of flowers: 1

217. *Dendrobium oligophyllum* Gagnep.

Thai name: Uang Khao Tok Prachin
เอื้องข้าวตอกปราจีณ
Distribution: Lower Northeast, Central, East
Flowering period: July–November
Characteristics: Greenish white flowers, lip white with three green keels, sidelobes triangular.
Size: 1.8 cm.
Number of flowers: 1

218. *Dendrobium pachyglossum* Par. & Rchb. f.

Thai name: Uang Khon Mu
เอื้องขนหมู
Distribution: Northeast, East, West, South
Flowering period: September
Characteristics: Sepals and petals light yellow with brownish longitudinal stripes, lip nearly white with yellowish green front and edges, green on back.
Size: 1 cm.
Number of flowers: 2–4 per node

219. *Dendrobium pachyphyllum* (Kze.) Bakh. f.

Thai name: Uang Song Bai
เอื้องสองใบ
Distribution: North, East, South
Flowering period: August–September
Characteristics: Sepals and petals white with purple lines, lip white with central greenish yellow or orange warts.
Size: 1–1.2 cm.
Number of flowers: 1

220. *Dendrobium palpebrae* Lindl.

Thai name: Uang Matcha
เอื้องมัจฉา
Distribution: North, Upper Northeast, East
Flowering period: February
Characteristics: Sepals and petals white, lip white with golden papillae.
Size: 3 cm.
Number of flowers: Up to 20
Scent: Apple fragrance

221. *Dendrobium parcum* Rchb. f.

Thai name: Uang Mai Kwat, Uang Kan Kiu
เอื้องไม้กวาด, เอื้องก้านกิ่ว
Distribution: North, Upper Northeast, West
Flowering period: September–February
Characteristics: Sepals and petals whitish to light greenish yellow, lip yellow with small purple dots on hypochile.
Size: 0.7 cm.
Number of flowers: 2–5

222. *Dendrobium parishii* Rchb. f.

Thai name: Uang Khrang Sai San, Uang Sai Nam Khrang
เอื้องครั่งสายสั้น, เอื้องสายน้ำครั่ง

Distribution: North, Upper Northeast, West

Flowering period: March–May

Characteristics: Sepals and petals purple, lip with two dark purple blotches, edges slightly ciliated.

Size: 3.8–5 cm.

Number of flowers: 1–3 flowers per node

223. *Dendrobium peguanum* Lindl.

Thai name: Nang Lom
นางลม
Distribution: North
Flowering period: January–February
Characteristics: Sepals and petals white, lip light brown with dark purplish brown veins.
Size: 1.3 cm.
Number of flowers: 5–8

224. *Dendrobium pendulum* Roxb.

Thai name: Mai Thao Rusi, Wai Pom
ไม้เท้าฤาษี, หวายปม
Distribution: North
Flowering period: February–April
Characteristics: White sepals and petals with lavender tips, lip pubescent with deep yellow blotch at base and lavender tip.
Size: 5–6.5 cm.
Number of flowers: 1–3 flowers per node

225. *Dendrobium primulinum* Lindl.

Thai name: Uang Sai Nam Phung
เอื้องสายน้ำผึ้ง
Distribution: North, Upper Northeast, West, South
Flowering period: February–March
Characteristics: Sepals and petals of about same width, light mauve, lip yellow with purple veins.
Size: 5–6.5 cm.
Number of flowers: 1 flower per node
Scent: Fragrant

226. *Dendrobium pulchellum* Roxb. ex Lindl.

Thai name: Uang Chang Nao, Uang Kham Ta Khwai
เอื้องช้างน้าว, เอื้องคำตาควาย
Distribution: North, Upper Northeast, Central, West, South
Flowering period: February–March
Characteristics: Creamy yellow with pink veins, pinkish lip with two big maroon blotches.
Size: 7.5–10 cm.
Number of flowers: 7–10

227. *Dendrobium salaccense* Lindl.

Thai name:–

Distribution: North, Northeast, Central, East, South

Flowering period: May

Characteristics: Greenish yellow flower with brownish purple marking on the lip.

Size: 1.3 cm.

Number of flowers: 1–2

228. *Dendrobium scabrilingue* Lindl.

Thai name: Uang Sae
เอื้องแซะ

Distribution: North, Northeast, East

Flowering period: December–February

Characteristics: White sepals and petals, midlobe of lip light yellow to orange, sidelobes with many green stripes.

Size: 2.5–3 cm.

Number of flowers: 1–3

Scent: Highly fragrant

229. *Dendrobium secundum* (Bl.) Lindl.

Thai name: Uang Praeng Si Fun, Uang Ngon Kai
เอื้องแปรงสีฟัน, เอื้องหงอนไก่
Distribution: North, Northeast, East, South
Flowering period: February–April
Characteristics: Rose-purple sepals and petals, orange or yellow lip. White flowers are rare.
Size: 0.6 cm wide and 1.8 cm. long
Number of flowers: 7.5–12.5-cm.-long inflorescence

230. *Dendrobium senile* Par. & Rchb. f.

Thai name: Uang Chani
เอื้องชะนี
Distribution: North, Upper Northeast, South
Flowering period: January–March
Characteristics: Yellow sepals and petals, lip with greenish yellow center.
Size: 3.7 cm.
Number of flowers: 1–2

231. *Dendrobium signatum* Rchb. f.

Thai name: Uang Kham Kiu
เอื้องคำกิ่ว
Distribution: North, Upper Northeast
Flowering period: February–April
Characteristics: White twisted sepals and petals with or without two purplish blotches.
Size: 5–6 cm.
Number of flowers: 1–4 flowers per node

232. *Dendrobium strongylanthum* Rchb. f.

Thai name:–
Distribution: North
Flowering period: September
Characteristics: Greenish yellow sepals and petals, sepals dark purple at base, epichile crenulated, deep maroon edges with greenish white tip.
Size: 1.4 cm.
Number of flowers: 10

233. *Dendrobium stuartii* Bailey

Thai name:–
Distribution: North, South
Flowering period: February
Characteristics: Pale greenish white flower with hairy lip.
Size: 2 cm.
Number of flowers: 1–2

234. *Dendrobium stuposum* Lindl.

Thai name:–
Distribution: North
Flowering period: May
Characteristics: Pinkish white sepals and petals, lip white with a yellow patch and yellow orange center, edges of epichile deeply ciliated.
Size: 1 cm.
Number of flowers: 2 flowers per node

235. *Dendrobium sukhakulii* Hort.

Thai name:–

Distribution: North

Flowering period: February

Characteristics: Bright yellow flowers, lip large with golden base.

Size: 2.5–3 cm.

Number of flowers: 6–7

236. *Dendrobium sulcatum* Lindl.

Thai name: Uang Champa Nan
เอื้องจำปาน่าน

Distribution: North

Flowering period: March

Characteristics: Yellow sepals and petals, lip boat-shaped, concave, papillae along edges.

Size: 3.5 cm.

Number of flowers: Up to 15

237. *Dendrobium sutepense* Rolfe ex Downie

Thai name: Uang Sae Mali
เอื้องแซะมะลิ
Distribution: North
Flowering period: February–March
Characteristics: White flower, lip white with yellow patch to the base, sidelobes with few brown lines.
Size: 2.5 cm.
Number of flowers: 1
Scent: Fragrant

238. *Dendrobium thyrsiflorum* Rchb. f.

Thai name: Uang Mon Khai
เอื้องมอนไข่
Distribution: North, Upper Northeast
Flowering period: February–April
Characteristics: White sepals and petals, lip bright yellow with orange base.
Size: 3–4 cm.
Number of flowers: 30–50
Scent: Delicate fragrance

239. *Dendrobium tortile* Lindl.

Thai name: Uang Kao Kiu Mae Sariang
เอื้องเก๊ากิ่วแม่สะเรียง
Distribution: North, West, South
Flowering period: February–April
Characteristics: Lilac-mauve sepals and petals, pale yellow lip with purple veins toward the base, petals twisted.
Size: 7.5 cm.
Number of flowers: 2–3 flowers per node

240. *Dendrobium trigonopus* Rchb. f.

Thai name: Uang Kham Pak Kai
เอื้องคำปากไก่
Distribution: North, Upper Northeast
Flowering period: February–March
Characteristics: Bright golden sepals and petals, lip golden color with greenish center and brown stripes.
Size: 3 cm.
Number of flowers: 2–3

241. *Dendrobium trinervium* Ridl.

Thai name:–
Distribution: South
Flowering period: October–January
Characteristics: Sepals and petals white, lip light orange tinted, sidelobes of lip semi circular with many purple dots along the median line on hypochile and three green lines on epichile.
Size: 1.5 cm.
Number of flowers: 1

242. *Dendrobium umbonatum* Seidenf.

Thai name:–
Distribution: East
Flowering period: August
Characteristics: Sepals and petals pinkish white, lip white with purplish red veins on sidelobes and yellow patch on midlobe.
Size: 2 cm.
Number of flowers: 3–4

243. *Dendrobium unicum* Seidenf.

Thai name: Uang Sai Si Saet
เอื้องสายสีแสด
Distribution: North, Northeast
Flowering period: February–May
Characteristics: Orange red sepals and petals, lip creamy yellow with reddish brown veins and three ridges callus along the center.
Size: 3 cm.
Number of flowers: 1–4 flowers per node

244. *Dendrobium venustum* Teijsm. & Binnend.

Thai name: Khao Nieo Ling, Uang Dok Ma Kham
ข้าวเหนียวลิง, เอื้องดอกมะขาม
Distribution: North, Northeast, Central, West
Flowering period: July–September
Characteristics: Pale greenish yellow sepals and petals, lip brownish yellow with brown stripes, epichile deeply fimbriated.
Size: 3 cm.
Number of flowers: 20

245. *Dendrobium virgineum* Rchb. f.

Thai name: Uang Nang Chee
เอื้องนางชี
Distribution: Northeast
Flowering period: June–August
Characteristics: Pure white flower, lip white with red or orange marking.
Size: 7.5 cm.
Number of flowers: 1–3

246. *Dendrobium wardianum* Warner

Thai name: Uang Mani Trai Rong
เอื้องมณีไตรรงค์
Distribution: North
Flowering period: January–April
Characteristics: White sepals and petals with purple tips, lip white with dark yellow toward base and purple toward tip, two maroon blotches on both sides.
Size: 5 cm.
Number of flowers: 1–2 flowers per node

247. *Dendrobium williamsonii* Day & Rchb. f.

Thai name:–
Distribution: North
Flowering period: March
Characteristics: Sepals and petals yellow, lip creamy white with dark orange patch to the base and orange papillae toward the front.
Size: 4.5 cm.
Number of flowers: 1

248. *Dendrobium wilmsianum* Schltr.

Thai name:–
Distribution: North
Flowering period: October–November
Characteristics: Light green flowers, upper side of the lip blackish purple.
Size: 1.1 cm.
Number of flowers: 10

(Flower forced open)

249. *Diploplora championi* (Lindl.) Hk. f.

Thai name:–
Distribution: North, Northeast, West, East, South
Flowering period: June
Characteristics: Yellow flower, lip white with brownish purple markings inside, tip of lip finely bifurcate.
Size: 1.5 cm.
Number of flowers: 3–5

250. *Diploplora truncata* Rolfe ex Downie

Thai name:–
Distribution: North, Upper Northeast
Flowering period: February
Characteristics: White flower, tip of lip truncate, the sack inside yellow with red and purple patches, callus yellow.
Size: 1.7 cm.
Number of flowers: 5–7

251. *Dorites pulcherrima* Lindl.

Ma wing (Left) Daeng Ubon (Right)

Thai name: Ma Wing
ม้าวิ่ง
Distribution: North, Northeast, East, West, South
Flowering period: May–October
Characteristics: Purple flower, petals as broad as sepals, lip dark purple. Diploid flowers 2n=38.
Size: 2–2.5 cm.
Number of flowers: 20

252. *Dorites pulcherrima* Lindl.

Thai name: Daeng Ubon
แดงอุบล
Distribution: Ubon Ratchathani, in the upper Northeast
Flowering period: June–August
Characteristics: White or light lavender to dark purple flower, lip dark purple. Tetraploid flowers 4n=76.
Size: 3.5–4 cm.
Number of flowers: 20–30

253. *Dorites pulcherrima* var. *chumpornensis*

Thai name:–
Distribution: South
Flowering period: June–August
Characteristics: White flower, petals with yellow patches at edges, sidelobes of lip brownish yellow, midlobe pinkish white.
Size: 3.5–4 cm.
Number of flowers: 10

254. *Drymoda picta* Lindl.

Thai name:–
Distribution: North
Flowering period: January
Characteristics: Light greenish white flower with dark reddish purple lip.
Size: 1.3 cm. wide and 0.7 cm. long
Number of flowers: 1

255. *Drymoda siamensis* Schltr.

Thai name:–
Distribution: North
Flowering period: February–March
Characteristics: Light green flower with brownish purple markings on sepals and petals, lip light green with longitudinal dark brown band.
Size: 0.7 cm. wide and 1.5 cm. long
Number of flowers: 1

256. *Epigeneium amplum* (Lindl.) Summerh.

Thai name: Kra Chiang, Si Thiang
กระเจี้ยง, ศรีเที่ยง
Distribution: North, Upper Northeast
Flowering period: November
Characteristics: Light yellow sepals and petals with dark brown striae to the base, lip dark reddish brown.
Size: 7 cm. long and 6.5 cm. across
Number of flowers: 1

257. *Eria acervata* Lindl.

Thai name:–
Distribution: North, Upper Northeast, West
Flowering period: May–June
Characteristics: Sepals and petals white, lip yellow with two red lines to the base.
Size: 1.5 cm.
Number of flowers: Up to 15

258. *Eria albidotomentosa* (Bl.) Lindl.

Thai name: Uang Kham Hin
เอื้องคำหิน
Distribution: Northeast, Central, East, South
Flowering period: June
Characteristics: Sepals and petals yellow inside, wooly white hair outside, lip yellow with brown markings.
Size: 3 cm.
Number of flowers: 10

259. *Eria amica* Rchb. f.

Thai name:–
Distribution: North, Northeast, East
Flowering period: March–April
Characteristics: Sepals and petals light greenish yellow with purple lines, lip with purple sidelobes and yellow epichile.
Size: 2 cm. wide and 1.2 cm. long
Number of flowers: 13

260. *Eria biflora* Griff.

Thai name: In–Chan
อิน-จัน
Distribution: North, Lower Northeast, West, South
Flowering period: June–July
Characteristics: Pale yellow flower, flower bracts light orange yellow, lip stronger yellow, papillous at edges.
Size: 0.3 cm. wide and 1.6 cm. long
Number of flowers: 2

261. *Eria bilobulata* Seidenf.

Thai name:–
Distribution: North
Flowering period: July
Characteristics: White flower, lip with clean white sidelobes and bright yellow midlobe.
Size: 1 cm.
Number of flowers: 10–12

262. *Eria bipunctuata* Lindl.

Thai name:–
Distribution: North
Flowering period: August
Characteristics: Sepals and petals white with pinkish tint, lip distally yellow, operculum light purple.
Size: 0.4 cm.
No of flowers: 18

263. *Eria concolor* Par. & Rchb. f.

Thai name:–
Distribution: North, Central, West, South
Flowering period: July
Characteristics: Flowers yellow, epichile strong yellow.
Size: 1.2 cm.
Number of flowers: 15

264. *Eria discolor* Lindl.

Thai name:–
Distribution: North, Upper Northeast, Central, South
Flowering period: April
Characteristics: Light brownish yellow flower with dark brown pentagonal lip.
Size: 1.7 cm.
Number of flowers: 4–5

265. *Eria javanica* (Sw.) Bl.

Thai name: Sawet Sukri
เศวตสุกรี
Distribution: North, West, South
Flowering period: August
Characteristics: White flower with red lines along sidelobes of lip, sepals with very light purplish dots.
Size: 4 cm.
Number of flowers: 20–30 cm. long inflorescence
Scent: Highly fragrant

266. *Eria marginata* Rolfe

Thai name:–
Distribution: Upper Northeast
Flowering period: May
Characteristics: White flower, lip white with purple edges on sidelobes, lighter purple edges and patch on midlobe, median keel hairy.
Size: 2 cm.
Number of flowers: 1–2

267. *Eria myristiciformis* Hook

Thai name:–
Distribution: North, West
Flowering period: August
Characteristics: Sepals and petals white, lip white with purple tint at base and sidelobes, distal part of lip yellow with two purple spots.
Size: 1 cm.
Number of flowers: 3–5

268. *Eria ornata* Bl. Lindl.

Thai name: Uang Tao Thong
เอื้องเต่าทอง
Distribution: South
Flowering period: September–October
Characteristics: Flowers dull chocolate brown, the large flower bracts bright orange red.
Size: 0.7 cm.
Number of flowers: 10 or more

269. *Eria pannea* Lindl.

Thai name: Phanni
พรรณี
Distribution: Widely distributed, except Central Thailand
Flowering period: March–April
Characteristics: Sepals and petals yellow orange, white wooly outside, lip reddish brown.
Size: 1 cm.
Number of flowers: 2–3

270. *Eria perpusilla* Par. & Rchb. f.

Thai name:–
Distribution: North, Lower Northeast, East, South
Flowering period: February
Characteristics: White flower, greenish at base of lip, operculum yellow.
Size: 0.3 cm.
Number of flowers: 7–8

271. *Eria siamensis* Schltr.

Thai name:–
Distribution: North, Northeast, East, South
Flowering period: July–August
Characteristics: Sepals white wooly outside, petals white, lip purple.
Size: 0.4 cm.
Number of flowers: 15-cm.-long inflorescence

272. *Eria spicata* (D. Don) Hand.-Mazz.

Thai name:–
Distribution: North, Northeast
Flowering period: June
Characteristics: Flower cream with pinkish tint, operculum dark purplish brown, lip with yellow tint.
Size: 0.6 cm.
Number of flowers: 25

273. *Eria sutepensis* Rolfe ex Downie

Thai name:–
Distribution: North, Upper Northeast
Flowering period: July
Characteristics: White flower, lip white with many red stripes on sidelobes, epichile yellow.
Size: 1.7 cm.
Number of flowers: 12

274. *Eria truncata* Lindl.

Thai name: Phuan–Phaeng
เพื่อน–แพง
Distribution: North, Upper Northeast, East
Flowering period: January–February
Characteristics: White flower, midlobe of lip purple edged.
Size: 2.2 cm.
Number of flowers: 1–2

275. *Esmeralda clarkei* Rchb. f.

Thai name: Ma Lai
ม้าลาย
Distribution: North
Flowering period: November
Characteristics: Yellow flower with dark brown bars, lip yellow with brown stripes.
Size: 6 cm.
Number of flowers: 4–5

276. *Eulophia andamanensis* Rchb. f.

Thai name: Mu Kling
หมูกลิ้ง
Distribution: Widely distributed
Flowering period: May
Characteristics: Greenish sepals and petals, lip white with three keels and reddish brown stripes and green edges, back of lip also green.
Size: 2.7 cm.
Number of flowers: 10

277. *Eulophia geniculata* King & Plantling

Thai name:–
Distribution: North
Flowering period: September
Characteristics: Light greenish yellow flower with brownish purple marking on lip.
Size: 1.5 cm.
Number of flowers: 10

278. *Eulophia graminea* Lindl.

Thai name: Chang Phasom Khlong
ช้างผสมโขลง
Distribution: Widely distributed
Flowering period: May
Characteristics: Sepals and petals pale yellowish green with darker veins, lip white.
Size: 3 cm.
Number of flowers: 15 or more

279. *Eulophia macrobulbon* Par. & Rchb. f.

Thai name: Wan Ung
ว่านอึ่ง
Distribution: North, Northeast, West
Flowering period: November–December
Characteristics: Sepals and petals greenish at base, purple toward tips, lip dirty green outside, grayish green on midlobe and tips of sidelobes, dark purple inside.
Size: 1.8 cm.
Number of flowers: Up to 50

280. *Eulophia pauciflorum* Guillaum

Thai name:–
Distribution: North
Flowering period: May–June
Characteristics: Sepals and petals green, lip white with pink hairs.
Size: 3 cm.
Number of flowers: 15

281. *Eulophia spectabilis* (Dennst.) Suresh.

Thai name: Wan Hua Khru
ว่านหัวครู
Distribution: North, Upper Northeast, East, West, South
Flowering period: April–May
Characteristics: Sepals dull reddish brown with some green, petals white apically with some reddish stripes to the base, lip white with purple veins.
Size: 1.5 cm.
Number of flowers: 10–15

282. *Flickingeria albopurpureum* Seidenf.

Thai name:–
Distribution: North
Flowering period: December
Characteristics: Pure white sepals and petals, lip white, sidelobes red–purple dotted, two wavy purple keels terminating above middle of mesochile, epichile white.
Size: 1.8 cm.
Number of flowers: 1

283. *Flickingeria compressa* Seidenf.

Thai name:–
Distribution: North
Flowering period: September
Characteristics: Flower white with red dots on hypochile, lip with two purple keels.
Size: 1.7 cm.
Number of flowers: 1

284. *Flickingeria fimbriata* (Bl.) Hawkes

Thai name:–
Distribution: Northeast, East, South
Flowering period: March
Characteristics: Sepals and petals creamy white with many small red dots, lip light yellow with red spotted sidelobes.
Size: 2 cm.
Number of flowers: 1

285. *Flickingeria ritaena* (King & Plantl.) Hawkes

Thai name:–
Distribution: North
Flowering period: June
Characteristics: Sepals and petals creamy white, hypochile and mesochile of lip purple, keels purple with yellow median line, epichile yellow.
Size: 1 cm.
Number of flowers: 1

286. *Flickingeria xantholeucha* (Rchb. f.) Hawkes

Thai name:–
Distribution: South
Flowering period: May
Characteristics: Sepals and petals creamy white, keels on lip distally yellow.
Size: 1 cm.
Number of flowers: 1

287. *Gastrochilus bellinus* (Rchb. f.) Kze.

Thai name: Sua Dam, Uang Tin Tao
เสือดำ, เอื้องตีนเต่า
Distribution: North
Flowering period: January–March
Characteristics: Light green sepals and petals with bold, deep purple blotches, midlobe of lip white with purple spots and deep yellow center, epichile long and hairy.
Size: 2.2 cm.
Number of flowers: 5 or more

288. *Gastrochilus bigibbus* (Rchb. f. ex Hk. f.) Kze.

Thai name:–
Distribution: North, Lower Northeast
Flowering period: October
Characteristics: Sepals and petals yellowish green, sack white with red-purple dots on edges.
Size: 2 cm.
Number of flowers: 10

289. *Gastrochilus calceolaris* (Buch.-Ham. ex J. E. Sm.) D. Don

Thai name:–
Distribution: North, Northeast, South
Flowering period: February
Characteristics: Sepals and petals greenish yellow with purplish brown spots, lip white with purplish red dots on yellow center.
Size: 1.5 cm.
Number of flowers: 3–5

290. *Gastrochilus minor* Seidenf.

Thai name:–
Distribution: North
Flowering period: January
Characteristics: Sepals and petals yellowish green with brownish red spots, lip white with yellow center.
Size: 0.8 cm.
Number of flowers: 10

291. *Gastrochilus monticola* (Rolfe ex Downie) Seidenf. & Smitin.

Thai name:–
Distribution: North, Upper Northeast
Flowering period: September
Characteristics: Sepals and petals yellowish green with brown patch, lip white with yellow center.
Size: 1.3 cm.
Number of flowers: 3–5

292. *Gastrochilus obliquus* (Lindl.) Kze.

Thai name: Sua Luang, Chang Rop Kho
เสือเหลือง, ช้างรอบคอ
Distribution: Widely distributed
Flowering period: November
Characteristics: Sepals and petals yellow with tiny red dots, lip white, sack white with yellow at base inside and purple edges.
Size: 2.7 cm.
Number of flowers: 20–25

293. *Gastrochilus psuedodistichus* (King & Plantl.) Schltr.

Thai name:–
Distribution: North
Flowering period: June
Characteristics: Yellow flower with brownish red spots, lip yellow with brown center.
Size: 0.8 cm.
Number of flowers: 6–10

294. *Gastrochilus rutilans* Seidenf.

Thai name:–
Distribution: Northeast
Flowering period: September
Characteristics: Sepals and petals yellow with dense brownish red dots, lip white, epichile yellow with brown dots.
Size: 1.3 cm.
Number of flowers: 5–6

295. *Gastrochilus suavis* Seidenf.

Thai name:–
Distribution: North, Upper Northeast
Flowering period: October
Characteristics: Sepals and petals yellowish green with red-brown spots, lip white, epichile with yellow patch and purplish red dots.
Size: 2.5 cm.
Number of flowers: 4–8

296. *Geodorum attenuatum* Griff.

Thai name:–
Distribution: North, Northeast, West, South
Flowering period: February
Characteristics: White flower, lip light yellow with yellow apex.
Size: 2 cm.
Number of flowers: 10

297. *Geodorum citrinum* Jacks.

Thai name: Wan Chung Nang
ว่านจูงนาง
Distribution: North, Upper Northeast, East, West, South
Flowering period: May–June
Characteristics: Yellow to greenish yellow flowers with red-purple longitudinal stripes on epichile.
Size: 3 cm.
Number of flowers: 5–10

298. *Geodorum purpureum*

Thai name:–
Distribution: North
Flowering period: March
Characteristics: White flowers with purple tint on edges of sepals and petals, lip white with purple tip and yellow patch distally.
Size: 1.7 cm.
Number of flowers: 9–10

299. *Geodorum recurvum* (Roxb.) Alston

Thai name:–
Distribution: North, Northeast, West
Flowering period: February
Characteristics: White flower, lip white with yellow patch and brown base.
Size: 2 cm.
Number of flowers: 18

300. *Geodorum siamense* Rolfe ex Downie

Thai name:–
Distribution: North, Upper Northeast, West
Flowering period: February
Characteristics: Light greenish yellow flower, epichile of lip with yellow warty disc.
Size: 2 cm.
Number of flowers: 4–5

301. *Grammatophyllum speciosum* Bl.

Thai name: Wan Phet Hung
ว่านเพชรหึง
Distribution: Upper Northeast, East, South
Flowering period: August
Characteristics: Yellow flower with dark brown markings, lip dark brown with three yellow ridges.
Size: 8 cm.
Number of flowers: 10

302. *Grosourdya appendiculata* (Bl.) Rchb. f.

Thai name:–
Distribution: Widely distributed
Flowering period: April–May
Characteristics: Sepals and petals pale yellow with red spots, lateral lobules of midlobe raising nearly as high to sidelobes.
Size: 1 cm.
Number of flowers: 1

303. *Habenaria carnea* N. E. Brown

Thai name: Wan Ya Nok We,
Lin Mangkon Bai Chut
ว่านยานกเว้, ลิ้นมังกรใบจุด
Distribution: South
Flowering period: September
Characteristics: Pinkish white sepals and petals, lip white with clefted apex.
Size: 2 cm. wide and 3.5 cm. long
Number of flowers: 10

304. *Habenaria chlorina* Par. & Rchb. f.

Thai name: Nang Ua Si Tong
นางอั้วสีตอง
Distribution: North, Upper Northeast
Flowering period: September
Characteristics: Yellowish green sepals and petals, lip yellow.
Size: 1.5 cm.
Number of flowers: 20

305. *Habenaria dentata* (Sw.) Schltr.

Thai name: Nang Ua Noi
นางอั้วน้อย
Distribution: Widely distributed
Flowering period: September–October
Characteristics: Pure white flower, sidelobes of lip fan–shaped, midlobe linear subulate.
Size: 1.8 cm.
Number of flowers: 15

306. *Habenaria furcifera* Lindl.

Thai name:–
Distribution: North, Northeast, Central, East, West
Flowering period: October
Characteristics: Greenish white flower, lip tripartite, spur as long as ovary.
Size: 2 cm.
Number of flowers: 10–15

307. *Habenaria hosseusii* Schltr.

Thai name:–
Distribution: North
Flowering period: September
Characteristics: Greenish white flower with 7–8 cm.-long spur.
Size: 2 cm. wide and 3 cm. long
Number of flowers: 12

308. *Habenaria lindleyana* Steud.

Thai name: Nang Krai
นางกราย
Distribution: Widely distributed
Flowering period: August–November
Characteristics: Pure white flower, midlobe of lip ovate-lanceolate, spur 4 cm. long.
Size: 2.5 cm. across
Number of flowers: 20

309. *Habenaria lucida* Wall. ex Lindl.

Thai name: Uang Hom Toei
เอื้องหอมเตย
Distribution: North, Upper Northeast, Central, East, West
Flowering period: August–September
Characteristics: Green flower with long spur.
Size: 0.5 cm. across
Number of flowers: Up to 40

310. *Habenaria malintana* (Blanco) Merrill

Thai name:–
Distribution: North, Northeast
Flowering period: September
Characteristics: White flower, lip lanceolate without sidelobes, no spur.
Size: 1.2 cm.
Number of flowers: Up to 10

311. *Habenaria medioflexa* Turrill

Thai name: Nang Ua Pak Foi
นางอั้วปากฝอย
Distribution: North, Upper Northeast, Central, East, South
Flowering period: September–October
Characteristics: Greenish sepals and petals, sidelobes of white lip deeply fringed.
Size: 2 cm. across
Number of flowers: Up to 30

312. *Habenaria rhodocheila* Hance

Thai name: Şang Hin, Lin Mangkon, Pat Daeng
สังหิน, ลิ้นมังกร, ปัดแดง

Distribution: Widely distributed

Flowering period: September–October

Characteristics: Dorsal sepal and lateral sepals green, the attractive part is the four-lobed lip of varied colors from light pink to dark pink, cinnabar to bright red, purple or yellow through orange.

Size: Lip is 2.5 cm. wide and 3 cm. long.

Number of flowers: Up to 15

313. *Habenbaria rostellifera* Rchb. f.

Thai name:–
Distribution: Northeast, East, West, South
Flowering period: September
Characteristics: White flower with pink tint, lateral sepals brown.
Size: 0.8 cm.
Number of flowers: 3-cm.-wide and 4.5-cm.-long inflorescence

314. *Habenaria rumphii* (Brogn.) Lindl.

Thai name:–
Distribution: Northeast, East, West, South
Flowering period: September
Characteristics: White flower, midlobe of white lip much longer than sidelobes.
Size: 0.8 cm.
Number of flowers: 3-cm.-wide and 4.5-cm.-long inflorescence

315. *Habenaria siamensis* Schltr.

Thai name:–
Distribution: North
Flowering period: August
Characteristics: White flower, sidelobe of lip filiform, spur clavate.
Size: 0.4 cm. wide and 1.2 cm. long
Number of flowers: 5

316. *Holcoglossum amesianum* (Rchb. f.) Christensen

Thai name:–
Distribution: North
Flowering period: October–January
Characteristics: Sepals and petals white with pink tinge, midlobe purple, lip white with yellow base and rose purple streaks, sidelobes white tinted with pale pink and small dots of darker rose pink at apex.
Size: 2.5–3 cm. across
Number of flowers: 10

317. *Holcoglossum kimballinum* (Rchb. f.) Garay

Thai name: Uang Nuat Pram Lam Dam
เอื้องหนวดพราหมณ์ลำดำ
Distribution: North
Flowering period: September
Characteristics: Sepals and petals very light pink, midlobe light pink with dense purple spots and four long purple lines and one short in the middle, sidelobes inside have dark brown spots and yellow tinted.
Size: 4 cm. across
Number of flowers: 5–7

318. *Hygrochilus parishii* var. *marriottiana* (Rchb. f.) Pradhan

Thai name: Lin Krabu
ลิ้นกระบือ
Distribution: North, Northeast, West
Flowering period: February–May
Characteristics: Brown or purplish brown sepals and petals with minute purple spots, base of petal almost white, lip purple or greenish purple.
Size: 4 cm.
Number of flowers: 5–10
Scent: Fragrant

319. Hygrochilus parishii Veitch & Rchb. f. Pfitz.

Thai name: Uang Nang Rung
เอื้องนางรุ้ง
Distribution: North
Flowering period: May
Characteristics: Greenish yellow sepals and petals with dark reddish brown blotches.
Size: 4 cm.
Number of flowers: 5–10

320. *Ipsea thailandica* Seidenf.

Thai name:–
Distribution: Northeast
Flowering period: December
Characteristics: Greenish brown flowers with light green trilobed lip, sidelobes raising, midlobe linear, operculum yellowish brown.
Size: 3 cm.
Number of flowers: 1–2

321. *Kingidium deliciosum* (Rchb. f.) Sweet

Thai name: Ka Ta Cho
กาตาฉ่อ
Distribution: North, Upper Northeast, East, West, South
Flowering period: May–June
Characteristics: Pale pinkish purple with darker tiny dots at base, lip white with pinkish purple lines on sidelobes and base of midlobe.
Size: 1.5 cm.
Number of flowers: 3–5

322. *Kingidium minus* Seidenf.

Thai name:–
Distribution: North, Upper Northeast
Flowering period: August–October
Characteristics: Sepals and petals yellowish white with purple lines, lip yellowish with purple blotches, sidelobes yellow.
Size: 1.8 cm.
Number of flowers: 2–3

323. *Lesliea mirabilis* Seidenf.

Thai name:–
Distribution: North, South
Flowering period: September
Characteristics: Brownish green sepals and petals, lip apex white with purple markings in the throat.
Size: 0.7 cm.
Number of flowers: 10 or more

324. *Liparis regnieri* Finet

Thai name:–
Distribution: North
Flowering period: May
Characteristics: Yellow flower with recurved yellow lip.
Size: 1 cm.
Number of flowers: 12–15

325. *Liparis siamensis* Rolfe ex Downie

Thai name:–
Distribution: North, Upper Northeast, West
Flowering period: September
Characteristics: Emerald green flowers with glossy dark green on the blade of lip, epichile broader than long.
Size: 0.8 cm.
Number of flowers: 20

326. *Liparis viridiflora* (Bl.) Lindl.

Thai name:–
Distribution: North, Northeast, Central, East, West, South
Flowering period: September
Characteristics: Yellowish green flowers, lip fat and recurved.
Size: 0.4 cm.
Number of flowers: 13-cm.-long inflorescence

327. *Ludisia discolor* (Ker-Gawl.) A. Rich.

Thai name: Wan Nam Thong
ว่านน้ำทอง
Distribution: East, South
Flowering period: January
Characteristics: White flower with yellow anther.
Size: 1 cm.
Number of flowers: 5–10

328. *Luisia brachystachys* (Lindl.) Bl.

Thai name:–
Distribution: North, East, West, South
Flowering period: April
Characteristics: Sepals and petals light green, lip purplish red.
Size: 0.8 cm.
Number of flowers: 2–3

329. *Luisia curtisii* Seidenf.

Thai name:–
Distribution: Upper Northeast, South
Flowering period: May
Characteristics: Sepals and petals whitish with purple tint, lip red purple.
Size: 1.5 cm.
Number of flowers: Up to 5

330. *Luisia filiformis* Hk. f.

Thai name:–
Distribution: North
Flowering period: April
Characteristics: Sepals and petals greenish yellow, lip dark brownish purple, division of hypochile and epichile nearly a straight line.
Size: 1.2 cm.
Number of flowers: 5

331. *Luisia macrotis* Rchb. f.

Thai name:–
Distribution: North, East
Flowering period: April
Characteristics: Sepals and petals pure light yellow, lip variable or darkly mottled.
Size: 1 cm. wide and 2 cm. long
Number of flowers: 1–2

332. *Luisia psyche* Rchb. f.

Thai name:–
Distribution: North, Northeast
Flowering period: June–September
Characteristics: Sepals and petals light greenish white, lip very dark purple with true sidelobes.
Size: 1.3 cm. wide and 2 cm. long
Number of flowers: 1

333. *Luisia thailandica* Seidenf.

Thai name:–
Distribution: North, Upper Northeast
Flowering period: May–June
Characteristics: Sepals and petals greenish yellow with purple tint, lip very dark purple, no true sidelobes.
Size: 2 cm. wide and 2 cm. long
Number of flowers: 1

334. *Luisia zollingeri* Rchb. f.

Thai name:–
Distribution: North, Northeast, Central, West, South
Flowering period: February
Characteristics: Sepals and petals greenish yellow, hypochile reddish purple, epichile green with purple flush.
Size: 0.7 cm.
Number of flowers: 12–14

335. *Malaxis acuminata* D. Don

Thai name:–
Distribution: North, West, South
Flowering period: July
Characteristics: Yellowish green flower, apex of lip split.
Size: 1 cm.
Number of flowers: 30

336. *Malaxis calophylla* (Rchb. f.) Kze.

Thai name: Haeo Mu Pa
แห้วหมูป่า
Distribution: North, Upper Northeast, South
Flowering period: July
Characteristics: Sepals and petals brownish pink, lip greenish yellow.
Size: 0.6 cm.
Number of flowers: 45

337. *Malaxis mackinonii* (Duthie) Ames

Thai name:–
Distribution: North
Flowering period: September
Characteristics: Purplish red flower, operculum greenish yellow.
Size: 0.5 cm.
Number of flowers: 4–5

338. *Malaxis ophrydis* (Koen.) Ormerod

Thai name:–
Distribution: North, Lower Northeast, East, South
Flowering period: December
Characteristics: Purplish brown flowers with darker purplish lip.
Size: 0.3 cm.
Number of flowers: 7-cm.-long inflorescence

339. *Malaxis orbicularis* (W. W. Sm. & J. E. Jeff.) Tang & Wang

Thai name:–
Distribution: North
Flowering period: July
Characteristics: Flowers blackish red, glossy.
Size: 1 cm. wide and 1.3 cm. long
Number of flowers: 20 or more

340. *Malleola dentifera* J. J. Sm.

Thai name:–
Distribution: North, Northeast, Central, East
Flowering period: July
Characteristics: Sepals and petals dirty yellow with red stripes, spur long and recurved at apex.
Size: 0.7 cm.
Number of flowers: 10

341. *Malleola insectiflora* (J. J. Sm) J. J. Sm. & Schltr.

Thai name:–
Distribution: Upper Northeast
Flowering period: July
Characteristics: Sepals and petals light yellowish green with reddish brown stripes, midlobe of lip white with recurved tip.
Size: 0.7 cm.
Number of flowers: 4–5-cm.-long inflorescence

342. *Mastigion fascinator* (Rolfe) Garay, Hamer & Siegerist

Thai name: Singto Nok Yieo Lek
สิงโตนกเหยี่ยวเล็ก
Distribution: Northeast
Flowering period: September–October
Characteristics: Light yellowish green sepals and petals with purplish brown lines, lip purple.
Size: 2.5 cm. wide, 16 cm. from tip of dorsal sepal to end of lateral sepals.
Number of flowers: 1

343. *Mastigion putidum* (Teijsm. & Binnend.) Garay, Hamer & Siegerist

Thai name: Singto Nok Yieo Yai
สิงโตนกเหยี่ยวใหญ่
Distribution: South
Flowering period: August–October
Characteristics: Lateral sepals greenish yellow with dense red spots, petals light green with tiny red dots.
Size: 0.9 cm. wide and 16–18 cm. long
Number of flowers: 1

344. *Micropera obtusa* (Lindl.) Tang & Wang

Thai name:–
Distribution: South
Flowering period: June
Characteristics: Sepals and petals pinkish white, sack yellow.
Size: 1 cm.
Number of flowers: 5–10

345. *Micropera pallida* (Roxb.) Lindl.

Thai name:–
Distribution: North, Upper Northeast, East, West, South
Flowering period: August–September
Characteristics: Flowers yellow, sepals outside with red-brown stripes.
Size: 0.8 cm. wide and 1.2 cm. long
Number of flowers: Up to 10

346. *Micropera rostrata* (Roxb.) Balakrishnan

Thai name:–
Distribution: North, Upper Northeast, Central
Flowering period: April
Characteristics: Flowers purple with a white tip of sack, operculum yellow.
Size: 1.2 cm.
Number of flowers: 25

347. *Microsaccus griffithii* (Par. & Rchb. f.) Seidenf.

Thai name:–
Distribution: East, South
Flowering period: July
Characteristics: Very small pure white flowers, in pairs.
Size: 0.3 cm.
Number of flowers: 2

348. *Nephelaphyllum tenuiflorum* Bl.

Thai name:–
Distribution: Northeast, South
Flowering period: July
Characteristics: Yellowish green flowers, epichile of lip tufted with papillae.
Size: 1 cm.
Number of flowers: 3–4

349. *Nervillea aragoana* Gaud.

Thai name: Bua Hua Dieo, Wan Phra Chim บัวหัวเดี่ยว, ว่านพระฉิม
Distribution: North, Upper Northeast, East, West, South
Flowering period: April
Characteristics: Brownish yellow sepals and petals with longitudinal brown stripes.
Size: 2.5 cm.
Number of flowers: 2–3

350. *Nervillea plicata* (Andr.) Schltr.

Thai name:–
Distribution: North, East, West, South
Flowering period: May
Characteristics: Light brownish green sepals and petals, lip white.
Size: 4.5 cm.
Number of flowers: 2

351. *Oberonia acaulis* Griff.

Thai name:–
Distribution: North, Lower Northeast
Flowering period: October
Characteristics: Yellowish green flowers, apex of lip bilobed.
Size: 0.3 cm.
Number of flowers: 20-cm.-long inflorescence

352. *Oberonia anthropophora* Lindl.

Thai name:–
Distribution: North, Lower Northeast
Flowering period: September
Characteristics: Sepals and petals pale reddish brown, lip deep red brown with paler lobes.
Size: 0.2 cm.
Number of flowers: 15–18-cm.-long inflorescence

353. *Oberonia falcata* King & Plantl.

Thai name:–
Distribution: North, Northeast
Flowering period: September
Characteristics: Pale green flowers, lip brownish orange, sidelobes much shorter than sepals.
Size: 0.2 cm.
Number of flowers: 50

354. *Oberonia rasmussenii* Seidenf.

Thai name:–
Distribution: North
Flowering period: September
Characteristics: Light orange sepals and petals, lip darker, flowers not touching each other.
Size: 0.1 cm.
Number of flowers: 18-cm.-long inflorescence

355. *Ornithochilus difformis* (Wall. ex Lindl.) Schltr.

Thai name: Soi Thong
สร้อยทอง
Distribution: North, Northeast, East, West, South
Flowering period: July–August
Characteristics: Yellow sepals and petals with thick reddish brown stripes, lip reddish brown.
Size: 0.5 cm. wide and 1 cm. long
Number of flowers: 25 or more

356. *Othochilus albus* Lindl.

Thai name:–
Distribution: North, East, West
Flowering period: June
Characteristics: White flowers with brown bracts, operculum brownish pink, lip with two yellow spots at base.
Size: 0.5 cm.
Number of flowers: 5-cm.-long inflorescence

357. *Otochilus fuscus* Lindl.

Thai name: Soi Raya
สร้อยระย้า
Distribution: North, Northeast, East, West
Flowering period: February
Characteristics: White flowers with long slender column.
Size: 1 cm.
Number of flowers: Up to 20

358. *Panisea tricallosa* Rolfe

Thai name:–
Distribution: North, Northest
Flowering period: October
Characteristics: Light yellowish flower with two yellow spots on the lip, no sidelobes.
Size: 1.7 cm.
Number of flowers: 1

359. *Panisea uniflora* (Lindl.) Lindl.

Thai name:–

Distribution: North, Northeast, East, West

Flowering period: August

Characteristics: Light greenish yellow flower with three orange spots on the lip, sidelobes distinct, operculum yellow.

Size: 1.5–2 cm.

Number of flowers: 1

360. *Paphiopedilum appletonianum* (Gower) Rolfe

Thai name: Rongthao Nari Khang Kob Kho Daeng
รองเท้านารีคางกบคอแดง

Distribution: East

Flowering period: March

Characteristics: Dorsal sepal light green with white border, lateral petals reddish pink, pouch green with red spots.

Size: 6 cm. across

Number of flowers: 1 (rarely 2)

361. *Paphiopedilum bellatulum* (Rchb. f.) Stein

Thai name: Rongthao Nari Fa Hoi
รองเท้านารีฝาหอย

Distribution: North

Flowering period: January–June

Characteristics: White flower with dark brownish purple spots.

Size: 6.5 cm.

Number of flowers: 1–2

362. *Paphiopedilum callosum* (Rchb. f.) Stein

Thai name: Rongthao Nari Khang Kop
รองเท้านารีคางกบ
Distribution: North
Flowering period: March–May
Characteristics: White sepals with green veins at base and purple at tip, dark purple warts with black hair on petals, pouch purplish brown.
Size: 8 cm.
Number of flowers: 1

363. *Paphiopedilum callosum* var. *sublaeve* (Rchb. f.) Cribb

Thai name: Rongthao Nari Muang Songkhla
รองเท้านารีม่วงสงขลา
Distribution: South
Flowering period: December–March
Characteristics: Flower usually somewhat smaller and darker than *P. callosum*.
Size: 7.5 cm.
Number of flowers: 1

364. *Paphiopedilum charlesworthii* (Rolfe) Pfitz.

Thai name: Rongthao Nari Doi Tung, Rongthao Nari Sri Sangwan
รองเท้านารีดอยตุง, รองเท้านารีศรีสังวาลย์
Distribution: Doi Tung, Chiang Rai in Northern Thailand
Flowering period: August–September
Characteristics: Dorsal sepal purplish pink with darker veins, petals yellowish brown with brown reticulate venation, lip yellowish brown with brown veins, staminode pure white.
Size: 6–7 cm.
Number of flowers: 1

365. *Paphiopedilum concolor* (Lindl.) Pfitz.

Thai name: Rongthao Nari Luang Prachin
รองเท้านารีเหลืองปราจีณ
Distribution: Northeast, Central, East, West, South
Flowering period: Year round, peak in June–August
Characteristics: Pale yellow flowers with tiny purplish spots, pouch also yellow.
Size: 5 cm.
Number of flowers: 1–3

366. *Paphiopedilum exul* (Ridl.) Rolfe

Thai name: Rongthao Nari Luang Krabi
รองเท้านารีเหลืองกระบี่
Distribution: South
Flowering period: January–April
Characteristics: Brownish yellow petals with brown spots, yellowish green dorsal sepal with big brown spots and broad white border, pouch brownish yellow.
Size: 5 cm.
Number of flowers: 1

367. *Paphiopedilum godefroyae* (Godefr.) Stein

Thai name: Rongthao Nari Luang Trang
รองเท้านารีเหลืองตรัง
Distribution: South
Flowering period: December–July
Characteristics: Creamy white flower with brownish purple striae, pouch white with minute brown spots.
Size: 5 cm.
Number of flowers: 1

368. *Paphiopedilum hirsutissimum* (Lindl. ex Hk. f.) Stein

Thai name: Rongthao Nari Luang Loei
รองเท้านารีเหลืองเลย
Distribution: Northeast
Flowering period: February–March
Characteristics: Dorsal sepal yellowish brown with green edge, petals twisted, purple inside and reddish purple outside, pouch yellowish brown.
Size: 10 cm.
Number of flowers: 1

369. *Paphiopedilum leucochilum* (Rolfe) Fowlie

Thai name: Rongthao Nari Luang Phang-nga
รองเท้านารีเหลืองพังงา
Distribution: South
Flowering period: August–October
Characteristics: Flower cream with brownish purple striae, pouch white with no spots.
Size: 6–8 cm.
Number of flowers: 1

370. *Paphiopedilum niveum* (Rchb. f.) Stein

Thai name: Rongthao Nari Dok Khao
รองเท้านารีดอกขาว
Distribution: South
Flowering period: March–July
Characteristics: White flowers with minute purple spots around the base of sepals, petals and pouch.
Size: 5.5 cm.
Number of flowers: 1–3

371. *Paphiopedilum parishii* (Rchb. f.) Stein

Thai name: Rongthao Nari Nuat Rusi, Rongthao Nari Chiang Dao, Rongthao Nari Muang Kan
รองเท้านารีหนวดฤาษี, รองเท้านารีเชียงดาว, รองเท้านารีเมืองกาญจน์
Distribution: North, West
Flowering period: June–July
Characteristics: Petals long and twisted, greenish yellow with dark purple spots near the base and solid purple toward the tip, warts and hair are present on the lower margin, dorsal sepal chartreuse striped with green, pouch brownish green.
Size: 7.5 cm.
Number of flowers: 2–4

372. *Paphiopedilum sukhakulii* Schoser & Senghas

Thai name: Rongthao Nari Pik Malaeng Po, Rongthao Nari Sukhakun
รองเท้านารีปีกแมลงปอ, รองเท้านารีสุขะกุล
Distribution: Northeast
Flowering period: August–October
Characteristics: Light green based petals with numerous purplish brown spots, pouch large with purplish brown veins.
Size: 10 cm.
Number of flowers: 1

373. *Paphiopedilum villosum* (Lindl.) Stein

Thai name: Rongthao Nari Inthanon
รองเท้านารีอินทนนท์
Distribution: North
Flowering period: January–February
Characteristics: Waxy greenish or brownish yellow, pouch yellowish brown.
Size: 12.5 cm.
Number of flowers: 1

374. *Papilionanthe biswasiana* (Ghose & Mukerjee) Garay

Thai name:–
Distribution: North
Flowering period: February
Characteristics: Lilac flower with purple long spur.
Size: 5 cm.
Number of flowers: 5

375. *Papilionanthe teres* (Roxb.) Schltr.

Thai name: Uang Mok
เอื้องโมก
Distribution: North, Upper Northeast, Central, South
Flowering period: March
Characteristics: Lilac sepals and petals, lip dark color with yellow sidelobes inside and lilac outside.
Size: 6 cm.
Number of flowers: 3–5

376. *Pecteilis sagarikii* Seidenf.

Thai name: Nang Ua Sakhrik
นางอั้วสาคริก
Distribution: Lower Northeast, Central
Flowering period: August–September
Characteristics: White sepals and petals, midlobe of lip white or bright yellow.
Size: 1.5 cm.
Number of flowers: Up to 10

377. *Pecteilis susannae* (L.) Rafin

Thai name: Nang Ua
นางอั้ว
Distribution: North, Lower Northeast, West, South
Flowering period: September
Characteristics: Dorsal sepal creamy white, lateral sepals light greenish yellow with white base, midlobe almost white, spur light yellowish green.
Size: 7 cm. across, midlobe linear 4 cm. long, spur 13 cm. long
Number of flowers: 8–10
Scent: Softly Fragrant

378. *Pelatantheria ctenoglossum* Ridl.

Thai name:–
Distribution: North, Upper Northeast, East
Flowering period: August–November
Characteristics: Sepals light yellowish brown with purple stripes, petals smaller and pink, lip white with yellow center.
Size: 1.2 cm.
Number of flowers: 1

379. *Pelatantheria insectiflora* (Rchb. f.) Ridl.

Thai name:–
Distribution: North, East, West
Flowering period: December–January
Characteristics: Green sepals and petals with reddish brown stripes, midlobe of lip red purple.
Size: 1.5 cm. across and 2.5 cm. long
Number of flowers: 1–3

380. *Peristylus affinis* (D. Don) Seidenf.

Thai name:–
Distribution: North
Flowering period: September
Characteristics: White flower, lip white and tripartite.
Size: 2 cm.
Number of flowers: Up to 25

381. *Peristylus tentaculatus* (Lindl.) J. J. Sm.

Thai name:–
Distribution: North
Flowering period: August
Characteristics: Light green flower, lateral sepals threadlike.
Size: 1.1 cm.
Number of flowers: 12

382. *Phaius flavus* (Bl.) Lindl.

Thai name:–
Distribution: North, Upper Northeast
Flowering period: August–September
Characteristics: Flowers greenish yellow, lip yellow with brown tip.
Size: 3 cm. across
Number of flowers: 10

383. *Phaius indigoferus* Hassk.

Thai name:–
Distribution: Upper Northeast, East, South
Flowering period: November
Characteristics: Sepals and petals brownish yellow, back white, lip yellow with brown stripes, spur short conical.
Size: 5 cm.
Number of flowers: 10

384. *Phaius mishmensis* (Lindl. & Paxt.) Rchb. f.

Thai name: Kluai Mai Dong
กล้วยไม้ดง
Distribution: Upper Northeast
Flowering period: November
Characteristics: Brownish purple flower, spur long and narrow.
Size: 5 cm.
Number of flowers: 12

385. *Phaius tankervilliae* (Banks ex L' Herit.) Bl.

Thai name: Uang Phrao
เอื้องพร้าว
Distribution: North, Upper Northeast, South
Flowering period: January–March
Characteristics: Reddish brown sepals and petals with white back, lip rose purple inside and whitish outside.
Size: 10 cm.
Number of flowers: 10–20

386. *Phalaenopsis cornucervi* (Breda) Bl. & Rchb. f.

Thai name: Khao Kwang On
เขากวางอ่อน
Distribution: North, Northeast, East, West, South
Flowering period: Year round, plenty in July–August
Characteristics: Greenish yellow petals and sepals with brown striae, pure color is rare.
Size: 3 cm. wide and 3.7 cm. long
Number of flowers: 2–3

387. *Phalaenopsis lobbii* (Rchb. f.) Sweet

Thai name:–
Distribution: West
Flowering period: February
Characteristics: White flower, lip white with two brownish yellow patches.
Size: 1.5 cm.
Number of flowers: 1–2

388. *Phalaenopsis lowii* Rchb. f.

Thai name:–
Distribution: West
Flowering period: October
Characteristics: Light purplish pink flowers with purple lip.
Size: 2.5–3 cm.
Number of flowers: 4–5

389. *Phalaenopsis parishii* Rchb. f.

Thai name:–
Distribution: North, West
Flowering period: April
Characteristics: White flower with purplish red lip.
Size: 1.4 cm.
Number of flowers: 1

390. *Pholidota articulata* Lindl.

Thai name: Uang To
เอื้องต่อ
Distribution: Widely distributed
Flowering period: May–June
Characteristics: Flowers white with light pink tint, hypochile of lip yellow.
Size: 1 cm.
Number of flowers: 15–20

391. *Pholidota bracteata* (D. Don) Seidenf.

Thai name:–

Distribution: North, Northeast, East, West, South

Flowering period: July

Characteristics: White flower, bracts brownish pink with many dense fine veins, lateral sepals free at base.

Size: 0.5 cm.

Number of flowers: 60 or more

392. *Pholidota convallariae* (Rchb. f.) Hk. f.

Thai name:–

Distribution: North

Flowering period: May

Characteristics: Pure white flowers with brown bracts.

Size: 0.5 cm.

Number of flowers: 20

393. *Pholidota imbricata* W. J. Hook

Thai name:
Distribution: Widely distributed
Flowering period: August
Characteristics: White flowers, lateral sepals connate near base.
Size: 0.6 cm.
Number of flowers: 15-cm.-long inflorescence

394. *Pleione maculata* (Lindl.) Lindl.

Thai name:–
Distribution: North, Upper Northeast
Flowering period: September–October
Characteristics: Sepals and petals white, margin of lip blotched with purple.
Size: 4.5 cm.
Number of flowers: 1

395. *Pleione praecox* (J. E. Sm.) D. Don

Thai name:–
Distribution: North, Northeast
Flowering period: November
Characteristics: Pinkish purple flower, lip white with purple markings.
Size: 3.5 cm.
Number of flowers: 3

396. *Podochilus cultratus* Lindl.

Thai name:–
Distribution: North, West
Flowering period: August
Characteristics: White flower with two purple blotches on lip edge.
Size: 0.4 cm.
Number of flowers: 2–4

397. *Polystachya concreta* (Jacq.) Garay & Sweet

Thai name:–
Distribution: North, Northeast, Central, West, South
Flowering period: August–September
Characteristics: Sepals green, petals light yellowish green, lip pale yellow.
Size: 0.6 cm.
Number of flowers: 12–15

398. *Pomatocalpa navaeta* J. J. Sm.

Thai name:–
Distribution: East
Flowering period: April
Characteristics: Sepals and petals brownish yellow with brown markings, lip yellow.
Size: 0.6 cm.
Number of flowers: 10–12 flowers per branch of the 40-cm.-long inflorescence

399. *Pomatocalpa spicata* Breda

Thai name: Chang Dam
ช้างดำ
Distribution: North, Lower Northeast, Central, East, West, South
Flowering period: February–March
Characteristics: Flowers yellow, sometimes without red, most often with red spots, midlobe heart-shaped.
Size: 0.5 cm.
Number of flowers: 5-cm.-long inflorescence

400. *Porpax elwesii* (Rchb. f.) Rolfe

Thai name:–
Distribution: Lower Northeast, East, South
Flowering period: July
Characteristics: White flower, no hair on outside of sepals and petals.
Size: 0.3 cm. wide and 0.7 cm. long
Number of flowers: 1

401. *Porpax lanii* Seidenf.

Thai name:–
Distribution: Northeast
Flowering period: May
Characteristics: Orange-brown flowers, sepals and petals outside with scattered short white hair.
Size: 1.8 cm.
Number of flowers: 2

402. *Porpax ustulata* (Par. & Rchb. f.) Rolfe

Thai name:–
Distribution: North, Lower Northeast, East, West
Flowering period: June
Characteristics: Reddish flower, back of sepals covered with short hair.
Size: 0.8 cm.
Number of flowers: 1

403. *Pteroceras leopardinum* (Par. & Rchb. f.) Seidenf. & Smitin.

Thai name:–
Distribution: North, Upper Northeast
Flowering period: February
Characteristics: Light orange-yellow sepals and petals with small brown dots, lip white with brown dots, tip of spur white.
Size: 1 cm.
Number of flowers: 6

404. *Pteroceras teres* (Bl.) Holt.

Thai name:–

Distribution: North, Northeast, Central, East, West, South

Flowering period: August

Characteristics: Sepals and petals greenish yellow with purple spots, spur white with dark purple apex.

Size: 1.2 cm.

Number of flowers: 7–8

405. *Rhyncostylis coelestis* Rchb. f.

Thai name: Khao Kae

เขาแกะ

Distribution: North, Northeast, East, West

Flowering period: April–June

Characteristics: Light blue sepals and petals with darker tips, lip dark indigo blue.

Size: 1.2–1.8 cm.

Number of flowers: 50 or more

Scent: Unpleasant fragrance

406. *Rhyncostylis gigantea* (Lindl.) Ridl.

Thai name: Chang Kra
ช้างกระ
Distribution: North, Northeast, West
Flowering period: December–February
Characteristics: White flowers with dark amethyst-purple spots of various sizes and density.
Sizes: 2.5 cm.
Number of flowers: Up to 50
Scent: Highly fragrant

407. *Rhyncostylis gigantea* var. *rubrum* Sagarik

Thai name: Chang Daeng
ช้างแดง
Distribution: Kabinburi in Western Thailand
Flowering period: December–February
Characteristics: Dark amethyst-purple flowers.
Size: 2.5 cm.
Number of flowers: Up to 50
Scent: Highly fragrant

408. *Rhyncostylis retusa* (L.) Blume

Thai name: Aiyaret, Hang Krarok
ไอยเรศ, หางกระรอก

Distribution: North, Northeast, East, West, South

Flowering period: May–June

Characteristics: Sepals and petals white with few purple spots, lip purple.

Size: 1.2–1.5 cm.

Number of flowers: 30–40-cm.-long inflorescence

409. *Rhytionanthos aemolum* (W. W. Sm.) Garay, Hamer & Siegerist

Thai name:–

Distribution: North

Flowering period: September–October

Characteristics: Brownish orange flower with purple lines, lip light pink.

Size: 9.7 cm. wide and 2.2 cm. long

Number of flowers: 5–6

410. *Rhytionanthos cornutum* (Lindl.) Garay et al.

Thai name:–
Distribution: North, Northeast, East
Flowering period: October
Characteristics: Yellowish brown flowers with longitudinal purple lines, lateral sepals forming a closed tube.
Size: 0.5 cm. wide and 3 cm. long
Number of flowers: 5–6

411. *Rhytionanthos spathulatum* (Rolfe ex Cooper) Garay et al.

Thai name: Singto Chon
สิงโตช้อน
Distribution: North, Upper Northeast
Flowering period: October
Characteristics: Yellowish brown petals and lighter dorsal sepal, lateral sepals spoon-shaped.
Size: 0.8 cm. wide and 1.7 cm. long
Number of flowers: 2–5

412. *Robiquetia pachyphylla* (Rchb. f.) Garay

Thai name:–
Distribution: North
Flowering period: May–June
Characteristics: Mauve flowers, spur cylindric.
Size: 0.4 cm. wide and 0.8 cm. long
Number of flowers: Up to 15

413. *Robiquetia spatulata* (Bl.) J. J. Sm.

Thai name:–

Distribution: North, Northeast, Central, West, East, South

Flowering period: April

Characteristics: Sepals and petals yellow with two reddish brown stripes and yellow midline, sack whitish yellow.

Size: 0.8 cm.

Number of flowers: 30

414. *Robiquetia succisa* (Lindl.) Seidenf. & Garay

Thai name: Uang Man Pu
เอื้องมันปู

Distribution: North, Lower Northeast, Central, East

Flowering period: June–August

Characteristics: Sepals and petals yellow with tiny red brown dots, spur dirty yellow with purplish brown tint, lip paler yellow with red markings.

Size: 0.7 cm. across

Number of flowers: 30

415. *Sarcoglyphis mirabilis* (Rchb. f.) Garay

Thai name:–
Distribution: North, Upper Northeast
Flowering period: April–June
Characteristics: Sepals and petals pinkish white with raised purple sidelobes of lip.
Size: 1 cm.
Number of flowers: 1

416. *Sarcoglyphis yunnanensis* Tsi

Thai name:–
Distribution: North
Flowering period: May
Characteristics: Sepals and petals white, lip purple with white apex.
Size: 1 cm.
Number of flowers: 10–13

417. *Schoenorchis fragrans* (Par. & Rchb. f.) Seidenf. & Smitin.

Thai name: Uang Chiu
เอื้องจิ๋ว
Distribution: North, Upper Northeast
Flowering period: April–June
Characteristics: Light purplish pink flowers, epichile with a single large callus.
Size: 0.3 cm.
Number of flowers: 20 or more

418. *Schoenorchis gemmata* (Lindl.) J. J. Sm.

Thai name:–
Distribution: North, Northeast, East
Flowering period: November
Characteristics: Pale amethyst flowers with white lip, dorsal sepal purple.
Size: 0.3 cm.
Number of flowers: Up to 20

419. *Seidenfadenia mitrata* (Rchb. f.) Garay

Thai name: Uang Nuat Phram เอื้องหนวดพราหมณ์
Distribution: North, Northeast, Central, West
Flowering period: March–May
Characteristics: White sepals and petals with purple tips, lip mauve.
Size: 1.2 cm.
Number of flowers: 30
Scent: Fragrant

420. *Smitinandia helferi* (Hk. f.) Garay

Thai name:–
Distribution: Lower Northeast, East, West, South
Flowering period: July
Characteristics: Sepals and petals greenish yellow, midlobe of lip white.
Size: 0.2 cm.
Number of flowers: 30

421. *Smitinandia micrantha* (Lindl.) Holtt.

Thai name: Khem Nu
เข็มหนู
Distribution: North, Northeast, East, West, South
Flowering period: June–February
Characteristics: Light pink flowers with dark color at sidelobes and midlobe of lip, sidelobes raising vertically.
Size: 0.6 cm.
Number of flowers: 20

422. *Spathoglottis affinis* de Vriese

Thai name: Luang Phitsamon, Luang Si Sa Ket
เหลืองพิสมร, เหลืองศรีสะเกษ
Distribution: Northeast, East
Flowering period: May–September
Characteristics: Cobalt yellow flowers, calli at base of midlobe fleshy, midlobe with long keel to apex.
Size: 3 cm.
Number of flowers: 2–5

423. *Spathoglottis plicata* Bl.

Thai name: Uang Din, Wan Chuk
เอื้องดิน, ว่านจุก
Distribution: East, South
Flowering period: August–November
Characteristics: Purple flowers with two bright yellow calli at base of midlobe.
Size: 3.7 cm.
Number of flowers: Up to 40

424. *Staurochilus dawsonianus* (Rchb. f.) Schltr.

Thai name: Uang Sua Phaeo
เอื้องเสือแผ้ว
Distribution: North, West
Flowering period: April
Characteristics: Sepals and petals pale green with brown markings, lip yellow, three lobes of midlobe rounded.
Size: 3.5 cm.
Number of flowers: 3–4

425. *Staurochilus fasciatus* (Rchb. f.) Ridl.

Thai name: Sua Khrong
เสือโคร่ง
Distribution: North, Northeast, East, West, South
Flowering period: April–May
Characteristics: Light yellowish green sepals and petals with brown markings, lip trilobed, white with few purple spots.
Size: 4–5 cm.
Number of flowers: 5–8

426. *Staurochilus loratus* (Rolfe ex Downie) Seidenf.

Thai name:–
Distribution: North
Flowering period: January
Characteristics: Sepal and petals yellow with brown spots, lip white, sidelobes of lip squarish truncate.
Size: 0.8 cm.
Number of flowers: 7–8

427. *Staurochilus ramosus* (lindl.) Seidenf.

Thai name:–
Distribution: North
Flowering period: March–April
Characteristics: Sepals and petals yellow with small brown spots, lip white, sidelobes of lip triangular acute.
Size: 0.8 cm.
Number of flowers: 4–5

428. *Stereochilus erinaceus* (Rchb. f.) Garay

Thai name:–
Distribution: West
Flowering period: June
Characteristics: Sepals with short hair outside, petals with two red stripes, sack purple.
Size: 0.8 cm.
Number of flowers: 2–3 on small plant.

429. *Sunipia andersonii* (King and Pantl.) P. E. Hunt

Thai name:–
Distribution: North
Flowering period: August
Characteristics: Sepals creamy yellow, petals and lip brown.
Size: 1.3 cm.
Number of flowers: 2

430. *Sunipia grandiflora* (Rolfe) P. E. Hunt

Thai name:–
Distribution: North
Flowering period: December
Characteristics: Sepals and petals light to dark purple, lip dark purple.
Size: 2 cm.
Number of flowers: 1

431. *Sunipia racemosa* (J. E. Sm.) Tang & Wang

Thai name:–
Distribution: North
Flowering period: March
Characteristics: Inflorescence pale green with purple tint on lip and edges of lateral sepals.
Size: 0.5 cm.
Number of flowers: 25

432. *Sunipia rimannii* (Rchb. f.) Seidenf.

Thai name:–
Distribution: North, West
Flowering period: February
Characteristics: Flowers greenish white with yellowish green patch on the lip.
Size: 0.8 cm. wide and 2 cm. long
Number of flowers: 4–5

433. *Tainia angustifolia* (Lindl.) Benth. & Hk. f.

Thai name:–
Distribution: North, Upper Northeast, East
Flowering period: September
Characteristics: Flowers yellowish brown with white lip and brownish yellow spur, lip with five long purple keels to the base, epichile purplish white.
Size: 3 cm.
Number of flowers: 8

434. *Tainia bicornis* Benth.

Thai name:–
Distribution: North
Flowering period: January
Characteristics: Sepals and petals greenish brown, lip bright yellow with two distinct keels along the low median keel.
Size: 1.7 cm.
Number of flowers: 3–4

435. *Tainia penangiana* Hk. f.

Thai name:–
Distribution: Lower Northeast, East, South
Flowering period: August
Characteristics: Sepals and petals greenish brown, lip white with yellow patch and keels.
Size: 3.5 cm.
Number of flowers: 10–17

436. *Tainia viridifusca* (Hook) Benth. & Hk. f.

Thai name:–
Distribution: North, Upper Northeast
Flowering period: January
Characteristics: Flower brownish yellow, lip whitish yellow with five raising keels, three middle keels are long to the base.
Size: 3.5 cm.
Number of flowers: 30

437. *Thecostele alata* (Roxb.) Par. & Rchb. f.

Thai name:–
Distribution: North, Upper Northeast, East, South
Flowering period: July
Characteristics: Sepals and petals yellowish green with brownish purple markings, lip white with dark pink marks.
Size: 1.2 cm.
Number of flowers: 10–12

438. *Thrixspermum amplexicaule* (Bl.) Rchb. f.

Thai name:–
Distribution: South
Flowering period: March
Characteristics: White flower with violet tint.
Size: 1.5 cm.
Number of flowers: 1

439. *Thrixspermum centipeda* Lour.

Thai name:–
Distribution: Widely distributed
Flowering period: July–September
Characteristics: Pale or deep yellow flower, lip lighter with a band of orange-red dots.
Size: lip 0.5 cm. wide, petals and sepals 3 cm. long
Number of flowers: 1 or 2 blooms at a time

440. *Thrixspermum sutepense* (Rolfe ex Downie) Tang & Wang

Thai name:–
Distribution: North, Upper Northeast, West
Flowering period: December
Characteristics: Greenish yellow sepals and petals, lip white with purple spots.
Size: 1.5–2 cm.
Number of flowers: 1

441. *Thrixspernum trichoglottis* (Hk. f.) Kze.

Thai name:–
Distribution: North, Northeast, Central, East, West, South
Flowering period: July–October
Characteristics: White flower, lip white with many orange dots, lip hairy.
Size: 1.2 cm.
Number of flowers: 1

442. *Trias intermedia* Seidenf. & Smitin.

Thai name:–
Distribution: Upper Northeast, East, South
Flowering period: June–July
Characteristics: Sepals and petals greenish white with seven purplish veins, lip greenish purple.
Size: 0.8 cm.
Number of flowers: 1

443. *Trias mollis* Seidenf.

Thai name:–
Distribution: South
Flowering period: December
Characteristics: Yellow sepals and petals, operculum forking into two arms.
Size: 1.3 cm.
Number of flowers: 1–2

444. *Trias nasuta* (Rchb. f.) Stapf.

Thai name:–
Distribution: Lower Northeast, East, South
Flowering period: October–November
Characteristics: Sepals greenish yellow, petals very small with purple tips, lip purple at proximal half, bright yellow towards tip.
Size: 2 cm.
Number of flowers: 1

445. *Trias oblonga* Lindl.

Thai name:–
Distribution: North, South
Flowering period: August–September
Characteristics: Sepals yellowish brown to dirty orange with seven thin brown lines, lip dark olive green with grass-green tip.
Size: 1.6 cm.
Number of flowers: 1

446. *Trias picta* (Par. & Rchb. f.) Parish & Hemsley

Thai name:–
Distribution: North
Flowering period: August
Characteristics: Sepals dirty yellow with many purple dots, petals dark purple, lip proximal part yellow with red dots, distal part reddish purple.
Size: 1.7 cm.
Number of flowers: 1

447. *Trichoglottis orchidea* (Koern) Garay

Thai name:–
Distribution: Upper Northeast, East, Central, West, South
Flowering period : February–May
Characteristics: Yellow sepals and petals with small brown patches, lip pure white.
Size: 1.7 cm.
Number of flowers: 1

448. *Trichoglottis tomentosa* Seidenf.

Thai name: Sua Sakhrik
เสือสาคริก
Distribution: North
Flowering period: July
Characteristics: Sepals and petals greenish yellow with brown blotches, lip white and hairy with purplish blotches.
Size: 2 cm.
Number of flowers: 1

449. *Trichoglottis triflora* (Guill.) Garay & Seidenf.

Thai name:–
Distribution: West
Flowering period: June
Characteristics: Greenish yellow sepals and petals, brown tinted inside, lip white with light purple dots.
Size: 0.5 cm.
Number of flowers: 2–3 at each node.

450. *Trichotosia dasyphylla* (Par. & Rchb. f.) Krzl.

Thai name:–
Distribution: North, Northeast, West, South
Flowering period: January
Characteristics: Hairy yellowish green flower, lip with two brownish purple patches on disc.
Size: 0.5 cm.
Number of flowers: 1

451. *Trichotosia velutina* (Lodd. ex Lindl.) Krzl.

Thai name:–
Distribution: Lower Northeast, West, South
Flowering period: June
Characteristics: Creamy white flower, lip base purple.
Size: 0.8 cm.
Number of flowers: 1–4

452. *Thunia alba* (Lindl.) Rchb. f.

Thai name: Chang Nga Dieo, Phothuki
ช้างงาเดียว, พอทุกิ
Distribution: North, Upper Northeast, East, South
Flowering period: January
Characteristics: Sepals and petals white, lip white with yellow center.
Size: 5 cm.
Number of flowers: 3–4

453. *Thunia bensoniae* Hk. f.

Thai name:–
Distribution: West
Flowering period: May
Characteristics: Sepals and petals purple, lip purple with yellow patch.
Size: 7 cm.
Number of flowers: 1

454. *Thunia bracteata* (Roxb.) Schltr.

Thai name:–
Distribution: North
Flowering period: May
Characteristics: Sepals and petals white, lip white with many purple longitudinal lines
Size: 6.5 cm.
Number of flowers: 2

455. *Vanda bensonii* Batem.

Thai name: Sam Poi Chomphu
สามปอยชมพู
Distribution: North, Upper Northeast
Flowering period: February–May
Characteristics: Light lavender sepals and petals with brown tessellation, lip rose purple.
Size: 4.3–5 cm.
Number of flowers: 5–12
Scent: Fragrant

456. *Vanda coerulea* Griff. ex Lindl.

Thai name: Fa Mui
ฟ้ามุ่ย
Distribution: North
Flowering period: July–December
Characteristics: Color varies from blue to bluish lavender, pink to reddish pink. Pure white is rare. Color may be solid or tessellated.
Size: 7.5–10 cm.
Number of flowers: 10–15

457. *Vanda coerulescens* Griff.

Thai name: Fa Mui Noi
ฟ้ามุ่ยน้อย
Distribution: North
Flowering period: February–April
Characteristics: Purple to lavender sepals and petals, lip dark bluish violet.
Size: 2–2.5 cm.
Number of flowers: Up to 15

458. *Vanda denisoniana* Bens. & Rchb. f.

Thai name: Sam Poi Khun Tan
สามปอยขุนตาล
Distribution: North, Upper Northeast
Flowering period: September
Characteristics: Color varies from ivory white, lemon yellow, golden yellow, yellowish brown to copper. No tessellation on flowers.
Size: 5–6 cm.
Number of flowers: 3–7
Scent: Fragrant

459. *Vanda lilacina* Teijsm. & Binnend.

Thai name: Khem Khao
เข็มขาว
Distribution: North, Northeast, East, West
Flowering period: January–March
Characteristics: White sepals and petals with lavender to purple tip, sidelobes of lip inside purplish dotted, front edge white.
Size: 1.8 cm.
Number of flowers: Up to 20

460. *Vanda liouvillei* Finet

Thai name: Sam Poi Nok
สามปอยนก
Distribution: North, Northeast
Flowering period: February–April
Characteristics : Flower yellow to brown with purplish brown tessellation, midlobe often fish-tail shaped.
Size: 2 cm.
Number of flowers: Up to 15

461. *Vanda pumila* Hk. f.

Thai name: Sa Laeng
สะแล่ง
Distribution: North
Flowering period: February–March
Characteristics: Creamy white sepals and petals, lip with purple streaks.
Size: 3 cm.
Number of flowers: 1–2
Scent: Fragrant

462. *Vanda testacea* (Lindl.) Rchb. f.

Thai name: Khem Luang
เข็มเหลือง
Distribution: North
Flowering period: September
Characteristics: Yellow flower with purple lip.
Size: 1.5–2 cm.
Number of flowers: 10

463. *Vandopsis lissochiloides* (Gaud.) Pfitz.

Thai name: Khao Phra Wihan
เขาพระวิหาร
Distribution: Upper Northeast
Flowering period: July
Characteristics: Sepals and petals strong yellow with reddish brown blotches inside, sidelobes of lip yellow, midlobe purple.
Size: 4 cm.
Number of flowers: 20–24

464. *Vanilla aphyllum* Bl.

Thai name: Thau Ngu Khieo
เถางูเขียว
Distribution: Lower Northeast, Central, East, South
Flowering period: October–November
Characteristics: Light green flowers, lip cream with numerous pink hair on disc.
Size: 3 cm.
Number of flowers: 1–3

Albino Variants

1. *Aerides falcata*

2. *Aerides flabellata*

3. *Cymbidium aloifolium*

4. *Dendrobium aphyllum*

5. *Dendrobium lituiflorum*

6. *Dendrobium pulchellum*

7. *Dendrobium secundum*

8. *Phalaenopsis cornucervi*

9. *Schoenorchis fragrans*

10. *Staurochilus loratus*

11. *Vanda liouvillei*

12. *Vanda coerulea*

13. *Vanda lilacina*

Anomalies

1. *Acampe papillosa*

2. *Brachycorythis sp.*

3. *Dendrobium anosmum*

4. *Dendrobium chrysotoxum*

5. *Dendrobium fimbriatum*

6. *Dendrobium findlayanum*

7. *Dendrobium findlayanum*

8. *Dendrobium lindleyi (semi double)*

9. *Dendrobium lituiflorum*

10. *Dendrobium primulinum*

11. *Dendrobium wardianum* 2n & 4n

12. *Natural hybrid of Dendrobium parishii and ?*

13. *Paphiopedilum exul (no synsepalum)*

14. *Pelatantheria ctenoglossum*

15. *Phalaenopsis cornucervi*

Index of Scientific Names

Index of Thai Names

ดรรชนีชื่อไทย

References

Cripp, P. 1987. *The Genus Paphiopedilum*. Portland, Oregon: Timber Press. pp 161–163.

Kamemoto, H., and Rapee Sagarik. 1975. *Beautiful Thai Orchid Species*. Bangkok: Aksornsampan Press.

Schelpe, S., and J. Stewart. 1990. *Dendrobiums: An Introduction to the Species in Cultivation.* Dorset: Orchid Sundries, Ltd.

Seidenfaden, G. 1975. *Orchid Genera in Thailand I–III: Calanthe, Cleisostoma, Coelogyne.* Dansk Bot. Ark. 29 (2-4).

Seidenfaden, G. 1976. *Orchid Genera in Thailand IV: Liparis* L. C., Rich. Dansk Bot. Ark. 31 (1).

Seidenfaden, G. 1977. *Orchid Genera in Thailand V: Orchidoideae.* Dansk Bot. Ark. 31 (3).

Seidenfaden, G. 1978. *Orchid Genera in Thailand VI: Neottioideae.* Dansk Bot. Ark. 32 (3).

Seidenfaden, G. 1978. *Orchid Genera in Thailand VII: Oberonia* Lindl. & *Malaxis* Sol. ex Sw. Dansk Bot. Ark. 31 (1).

Seidenfaden, G. 1979. *Orchid Genera in Thailand VIII: Bulbophyllum* Thou. Dansk Bot. Ark. 33 (3).

Seidenfaden, G. 1980. *Orchid General in Thailand IX: Flickingeria* Hawkes & *Epigeneium* Gagnep. Dansk Bot. Ark. 34 (1).

Seidenfaden, G. 1982. *Orchid Genera in Thailand X: Trichotosia* Bl. & *Eria* Lindl. Opera Bot. 62.

Seidenfaden, G. 1983. *Orchid Genera in Thailand XI: Cymbidieae Pfitz.* Opera Bot. 72.

Seidenfaden, G. 1985. *Orchid Genera in Thailand XII: Dendrobium Sw.* Opera Bot. 83.

Seidenfaden, G. 1986. *Orchid Genera in Thailand XIII: Thirty-three Epidendroid Genera.* Opera Bot. 89.

Seidenfaden, G. 1988. *Orchid Genera in Thailand XIV: Fifty-nine Vandoid Genera.* Opera Bot. 95.

Seidenfaden, G. 1995. *Contribution to the Orchid Flora of Thailand XII.* Opera Bot. 124.

Seidenfaden, G. 1997. *Contribution to the Orchid Flora of Thailand XIII.* Olsen & Olsen.

Vaddhanaphuti, N. 1992. *A Field Guide to the Wild Orchids of Thailand*. Chiang Mai: Silkworm Books.

เต็ม สมิตินันท์. 2523. *ชื่อพรรณไม้แห่งประเทศไทย: ชื่อพฤกษศาสตร์-ชื่อพื้นเมือง.* กรุงเทพฯ: กรมป่าไม้.

ระพี สาคริก. 2516. *การเพาะปลูกกล้วยไม้ในสภาพแวดล้อมของประเทศไทย.* กรุงเทพฯ: โรงพิมพ์ชวนพิมพ์.

สมศักดิ์ รักไพบูลย์สมบัติ. 2535. *ทำเนียบกล้วยไม้ไทย.* เชียงใหม่: สุริวงศ์บุ๊คเซนเตอร์.